The Borden Tragedy

NBM ComicsLit

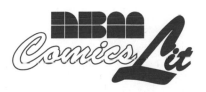

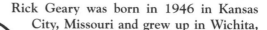

Rick Geary was born in 1946 in Kansas City, Missouri and grew up in Wichita, Kansas. He graduated from the University of Kansas in Lawrence, where his first cartoons were published in the University Daily Kansan.

He worked as staff artist for two weekly papers in Wichita before moving to San Diego in 1975.

He began work in comics in 1977 and was for thirteen years a contributor to the Funny Pages of National Lampoon. His comic stories have also been published in Heavy Metal, Dark Horse Comics and the DC Comics/Paradox Press Big Books. His early comic work has been collected in Housebound with Rick Geary from Fantagraphics Books.

During a four-year stay in New York, his illustrations appeared regularly in The New York Times Book Review. His illustration work has also been seen in MAD, Spy, Rolling Stone, The Los Angeles Times, and American Libraries.

He has written and illustrated three children's books based on The Mask for Dark Horse and two Spider-Man children's books for Marvel. His children's comic Society of Horrors ran in Disney Adventures magazine from 1999 to 2006. He is currently the artist for the new series of Gumby comics, written by Bob Burden.

His graphic novels include three adaptations for CLASSICS ILLUSTRATED. In 2007, he wrote and illustrated J. Edgar Hoover: A Graphic Biography for Farrar, Straus and Giroux.

In 2007, after more than thirty years in San Diego, he and his wife Deborah moved to the town of Carrizozo, New Mexico.

The Borden Tragedy

ANDREW AND ABBY BORDEN

EMMA

A Memoir of
the Infamous Double Murder
at Fall River, Mass.
1892

LIZZIE

Adapted and Illustrated by
Rick Geary

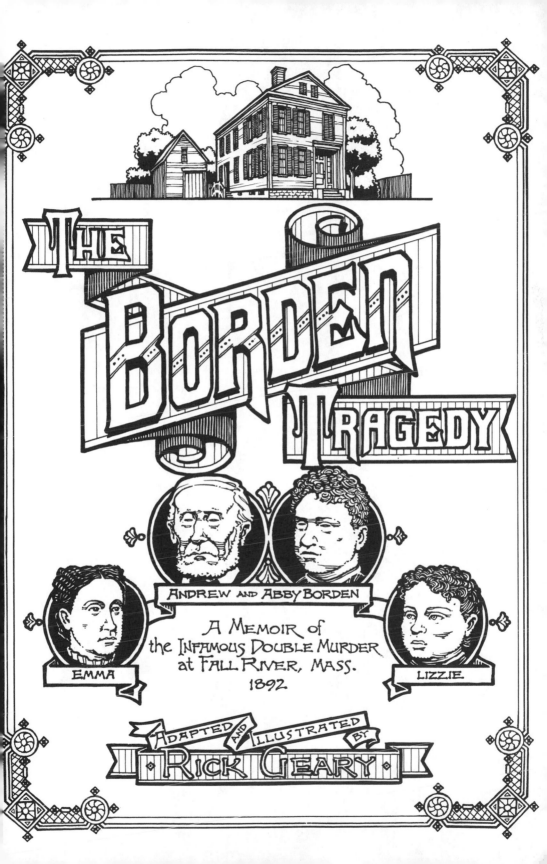

Also available by Geary:
A Treasury of Victorian Murder:
Jack The Ripper, pb.: $9.95
The Murder of Abraham Lincoln, pb.: $9.95
hc.: $15.95
The Fatal Bullet, pb.: $9.95
The Mystery of Mary Rogers
hc.: $15.95
The Beast of Chicago, pb.: $9.95
The Case of Madeleine Smith
pb.: $8.95, hc.: $15.95
The Bloody Benders
pb.: $9.95, hc.: $15.95
A Treasury of XXth Century Murder:
The Lindbergh Child
pb.: $9.95, hc.: $15.95

P&H: $4 1st item, $1 each addt'l.

We have over 200 titles, write
for our color catalog:
NBM
40 Exchange Pl., Suite 1308,
New York, NY 10005

www.nbmpublishing.com

ISBN-10: 1-56163-189-2
ISBN-13: 978-1-56163-189-6
©1997 Rick Geary

7 6

Comicslit is an imprint
and trademark of

nbm

NANTIER • BEALL • MINOUSTCHINE
Publishing inc.
new york

INTRODUCTION

The account presented in these pages of 19th Century America's most famous murder case is excerpted and adapted from the unpublished memoirs of a (thus far) unknown lady of Fall River, Massachusetts. Since the typewritten, unedited manuscript came to light at a 1990 estate sale, its provenance has been established to a satisfying degree. As part of the contents of an unopened trunk, it resided since the turn of the century in the basement of a private archive in Boston.

In the years since the public release of the memoirs, speculation has been lively among Bordenologists as to the identity of their mysterious authoress, who drops tantalizing hints throughout the text. Her apparent intimacy with the Borden family and her knowledge of Fall River's history and social structure have prompted theorists to champion several candidates, even the ambiguous and elusive "family friend," Miss Alice Russell. No hard evidence as yet points to any individual.

BIBLIOGRAPHY

The facts contained in the memoirs have been found to conform to the following sources:

Brown, Arnold R. *Lizzie Borden: The Legend, the Truth, the Final Chapter*. Nashville: Rutledge Hill Press, 1991.

Flynn, Robert A., *Lizzie Borden and the Mysterious Axe*. Portland, Maine: King Phillip Publishing Co., 1992.

Infamous Murders. London: Verdict Press, 1975.

Kent, David, *Forty Whacks: New Evidence in the Life and Legend of Lizzie Borden*. Emmaus, Pennsylvania: Yankee Books, 1992.

Kent, David, and Robert A. Flynn, *The Lizzie Borden Sourcebook*. Boston: Branden Publishing Co., 1992.

Lincoln, Victoria, *A Private Disgrace: Lizzie Borden by Daylight*. New York: G.P. Putnam's Sons, 1967.

Pearson, Edmund, "The Borden Case." Reprinted in *Unsolved!*, Richard Glyn Jones, ed. New York: Peter Bedrick Books, 1987.

Samuels, Charles and Louise, *The Girl in the House of Hate*. Mattituck, New York: Aeonian Press, Inc., 1953.

Spiering, Frank. *Lizzie*. New York: Random House, 1984.

Williams, Joyce G., J. Eric Smithburn and M. Jeanne Peterson, eds., Lizzie Borden: *A Casebook of Family and Crime in the 1890's*. Bloomington, Indiana, T.I.S. Publications, 1980.

Wilson Colin. *True Crime 2*. New York: Carroll and Graf, 1990.

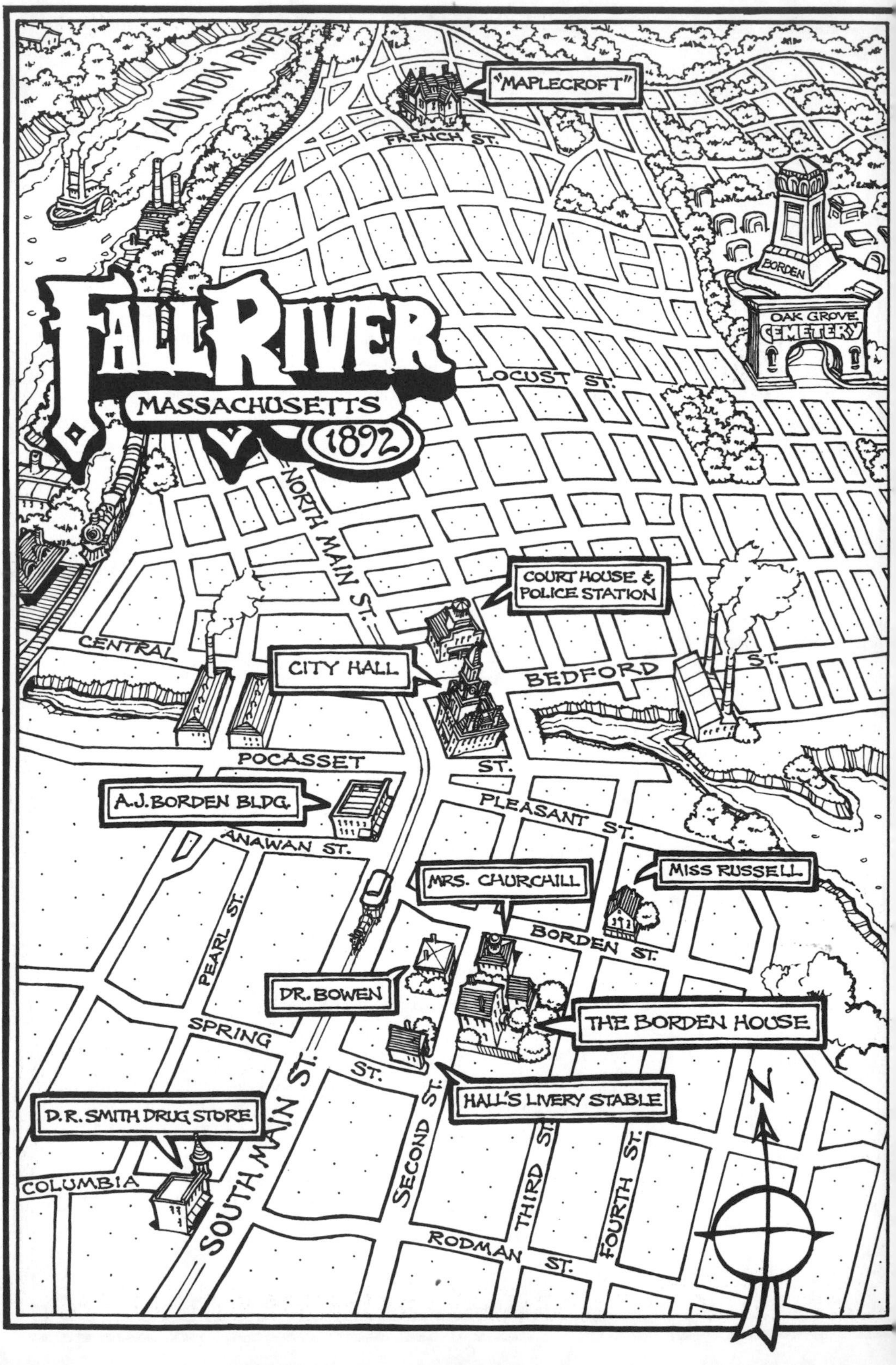

FALL RIVER
MASSACHUSETTS
1892
TAUNTON RIVER
"MAPLECROFT"
FRENCH ST.
BORDEN
OAK GROVE CEMETERY
LOCUST ST.
NORTH MAIN ST.
COURT HOUSE & POLICE STATION
CENTRAL
CITY HALL
BEDFORD ST.
POCASSET ST.
A.J. BORDEN BLDG.
PLEASANT ST.
ANAWAN ST.
MRS. CHURCHILL
MISS RUSSELL
PEARL ST.
BORDEN ST.
DR. BOWEN
SPRING ST.
THE BORDEN HOUSE
SOUTH MAIN ST.
SECOND ST.
HALL'S LIVERY STABLE
D.R. SMITH DRUG STORE
COLUMBIA
THIRD ST.
FOURTH ST.
RODMAN ST.
N

THE GRIM AND SEETHING SUMMER OF 1892 WILL NEVER DEPART MY MEMORY . . .

NOR, I DARESAY, WILL IT BE EVER FORGOT BY THE GOOD CITIZENS OF FALL RIVER.

WITH TEMPERATURES ABOVE 100 DEGREES DAILY, THE PACE OF COMMERCIAL LIFE SLOWED TO A CRAWL.

HORSES COLLAPSED WHILE ATTEMPTING TO SCALE THE STEEPEST STREETS.

ON THAT STIFLING MORNING OF AUGUST 4, OUR 75,000 RESIDENTS WERE GOING ABOUT THEIR BUSINESS WITH NO INKLING THAT THEIR LIVES WERE ABOUT TO CHANGE UTTERLY AND FOREVER.

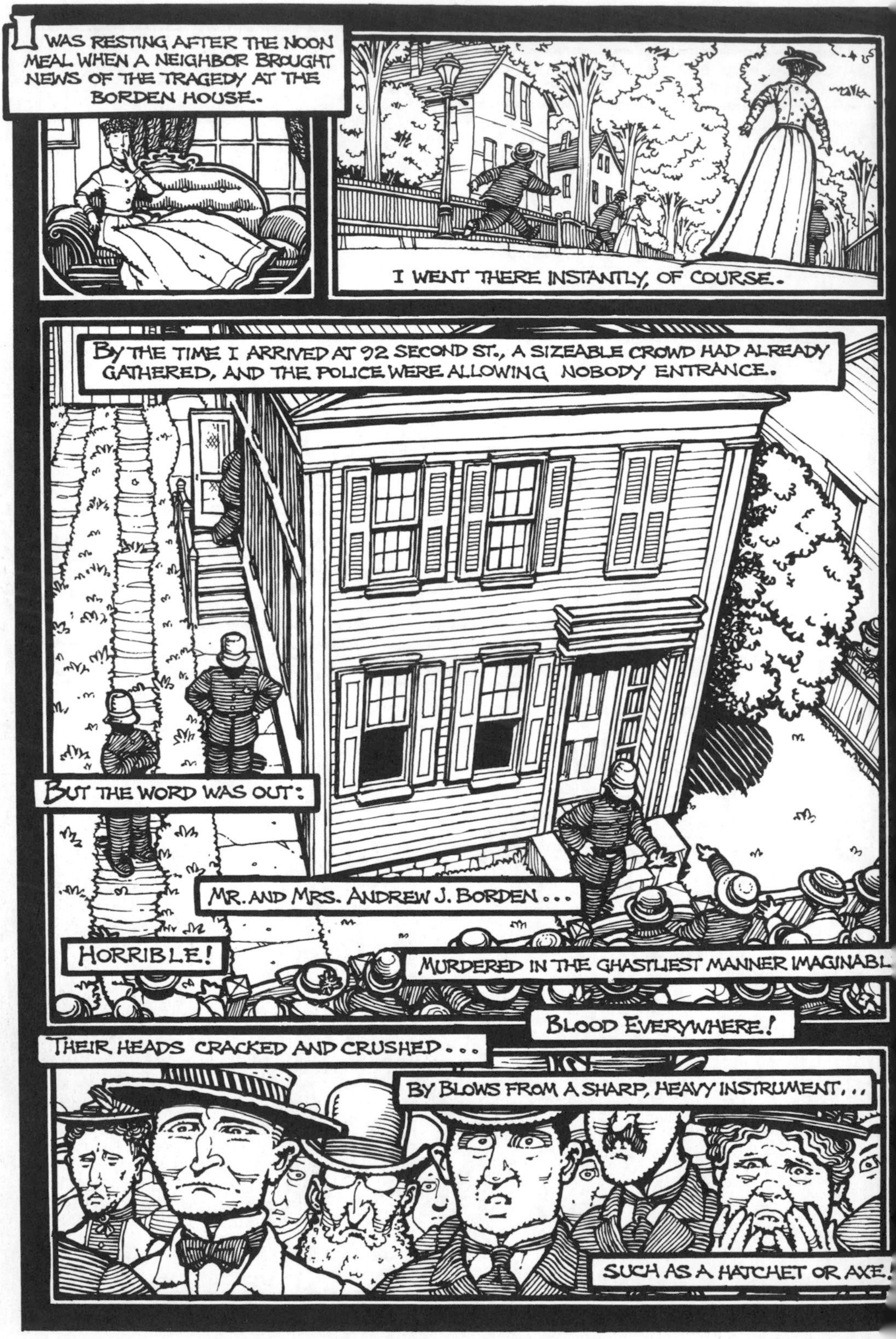
I WAS RESTING AFTER THE NOON MEAL WHEN A NEIGHBOR BROUGHT NEWS OF THE TRAGEDY AT THE BORDEN HOUSE.
I WENT THERE INSTANTLY, OF COURSE.
BY THE TIME I ARRIVED AT 92 SECOND ST., A SIZEABLE CROWD HAD ALREADY GATHERED, AND THE POLICE WERE ALLOWING NOBODY ENTRANCE.
BUT THE WORD WAS OUT:
MR. AND MRS. ANDREW J. BORDEN...
HORRIBLE!
MURDERED IN THE GHASTLIEST MANNER IMAGINABL
BLOOD EVERYWHERE!
THEIR HEADS CRACKED AND CRUSHED...
BY BLOWS FROM A SHARP, HEAVY INSTRUMENT...
SUCH AS A HATCHET OR AXE!

AT THAT TIME, APART FROM THE TWO VICTIMS, I KNEW THERE TO BE FOUR PERSONS RESIDENT IN THE BORDEN HOUSE —

ANDREW BORDEN

ABBY, HIS 2ND WIFE

THE IRISH HOUSEMAID BRIDGET

TWO DAUGHTERS BY HIS LATE 1ST WIFE: EMMA, THE ELDER...

AND THE YOUNGER, LIZZIE.

JOHN V. MORSE, A RELATION VISITING FROM NEW BEDFORD

I HAD THEN KNOWN THE BORDEN FAMILY FOR PERHAPS A SCORE OF YEARS, THE DAUGHTER LIZZIE BEING OF MY OWN AGE.

AS YOUNG LADIES, WE OFTEN ATTENDED THE SAME SOCIAL FUNCTIONS, AND HAD OCCASION, NOW AND THEN, TO SHARE OUR MOST INTIMATE THOUGHTS.

NONE OF THIS, HOWEVER, COULD GAIN ME ENTRANCE TO THE BORDEN HOUSE ON THAT DAY.

FOR THE REST OF THE AFTERNOON, POLICEMEN BY THE DOZENS TROOPED IN AND OUT.

LIGHTS IN THE HOUSE BURNED INTO THE SWELTERING NIGHT. "WHAT CAN BE HAPPENING IN THERE?" WE ALL WONDERED.

OVER THE NEXT SEVERAL DAYS, THE NORMAL ACTIVITY OF FALL RIVER GROUND TO A HALT, AS THE NEWS SPREAD FAR AND WIDE.

ANDREW BORDEN WAS OF COURSE WELL KNOWN FOR HIS STERN AND PENURIOUS WAYS. HE WAS MOURNED AS ONE OF THE TOWN'S LEADING CITIZENS.

JOURNALISTS FROM AS FAR AS BOSTON AND NEW YORK PROVED ASSIDUOUS IN FERRETING OUT RUMORS AND ACCUSATIONS.

AS WE AWAITED AN ARREST, DEBATE ON THE STREETS WAS LIVELY.

NINETEEN BLOWS!

NO... TWENTY-ONE!

CONSENSUS OF OPINION AT FIRST HELD THE KILLER TO BE ONE OF THE FAST-BREEDING PORTUGESE FROM THE SOUTH END OF TOWN...

OR, FAILING THAT, ONE OF THE VIOLENT-TEMPERED IRISH — PERHAPS THE FAMILY'S OWN HOUSEMAID!

LIZZIE BORDEN HERSELF WAS ALSO UNDER A CLOUD:

WORD SPREAD THAT SHE HAD ATTEMPTED TO PURCHASE POISON FROM A LOCAL DRUGGIST ON THE DAY BEFORE THE CRIMES.

AND WHAT OF THE SHADOWY CHARACTER OF JOHN V. MORSE (BROTHER OF ANDREW'S LATE FIRST WIFE AND UNCLE TO EMMA AND LIZZIE)?

SUPPOSEDLY, HE WAS PAYING A CALL ACROSS TOWN DURING THE TIME OF THE MURDERS.

ABOVE ALL, THE VISION OF A RAVING MAD-MAN AT LARGE IN THE COUNTRYSIDE AND SWINGING A BLOOD-SMEARED AXE, HAUNTED OUR DREAMS AND PRE-OCCUPIED OUR WAKING HOURS.

ON AUGUST 9-11, AN INQUEST, CLOSED TO THE PUBLIC, WAS CONDUCTED, DURING WHICH THE STATEMENTS OF ALL THOSE INVOLVED WERE PUT INTO LEGAL RECORD.

UPON ITS ADJOURNMENT, LIZZIE BORDEN WAS PLACED UNDER ARREST FOR THE MURDERS OF HER FATHER AND STEPMOTHER.

THIS ACTION, WE WERE TOLD, WAS BASED UPON SEVERAL INCONSISTENCIES IN HER TESTIMONY ... IN ADDITION TO THE FACT THAT NOBODY ELSE SEEMED TO HAVE HAD THE OPPORTUNITY.

I WAS THUNDER-STRUCK! HOW COULD THIS WELL-BRED, CHURCHGOING LADY, TO WHOSE NAME NO BREATH OF SCANDAL WAS EVER ATTACHED — AND WHOM I HAD ONCE CONSIDERED CONFIDANTE — HAVE COMMITTED AN ACT OF SUCH STUNNING BRUTALITY?

The Fall

MISS BORDEN ARRESTED.

CHARGED WITH MURDERING HER FATHER AND HIS WIFE

STARTLING TESTIMONY

TAKEN TO TAUNTON

IF TRUE, THERE WAS MORE RAGE AND HATRED WITHIN THAT HOUSE THAN I COULD EVER HAVE IMAGINED!

ON THAT DAY, I DETERMINED TO MYSELF THAT I HAD TO KNOW THE TRUTH OF WHAT HAPPENED ON THE MORNING OF AUGUST 4 ... AND THAT I WOULD FIND IT OUT, EVEN IF I HAD TO PLAY "DETECTIVE."

THE ACCOUNT I PRESENT IN THESE PAGES OF THE INFAMOUS BORDEN MURDERS HAS BEEN ASSEMBLED FROM MY OWN RESEARCH, INCLUDING CONVERSATIONS WITH THE PARTICIPANTS IN THE DRAMA, AS WELL AS THE PUBLIC RECORD OF THE LEGAL PROCEEDINGS AGAINST LIZZIE BORDEN.

THE CONFLICTS WITHIN THE BORDEN FAMILY, I FOUND, HAD THEIR ORIGINS LONG BEFORE I KNEW LIZZIE — AND LONG BEFORE THEY OCCUPIED THE HOUSE ON SECOND STREET.

THEIR NAME, OF COURSE, HAS ALWAYS BEEN A CRUCIAL ONE IN FALL RIVER, AS ONE OF THE HANDFUL OF FAMILIES THAT ESTABLISHED THE COTTON MILLS AND AMASSED GREAT WEALTH OVER THE YEARS.

HOWEVER, BY THE TIME OF ANDREW BORDEN'S BIRTH, HIS BRANCH OF THE FAMILY HAD FALLEN INTO POVERTY AND DISREPUTE...

FROM WHICH HE WAS FORCED TO CLIMB BY DINT OF THRIFT, SHREWDNESS AND HARD LABOR.

IN 1845, HE MARRIED A LOCAL WOMAN, SARAH MORSE.

THEIR UNION PRODUCED TWO DAUGHTERS: EMMA, BORN IN 1851...

AND LIZZIE, BORN IN 1860.

SARAH PASSED ON IN 1863...

AND TWO YEARS LATER, ANDREW MARRIED ABBY DURFEE GRAY, THE SPINSTER DAUGHTER OF ANOTHER PROMINENT FALL RIVER FAMILY.

BY THIS TIME, ANDREW HAD WORKED FOR MANY YEARS AS FALL RIVER'S UNDERTAKER.

IN ADDITION, THE INCOME FROM HIS MANY PROPERTIES AND INVESTMENTS, PUT HIM AMONG THE TOWN'S WEALTHIEST CITIZENS.

A.J. BORDEN BLDG. — S. MAIN ST.

IN 1871, WHEN HE PURCHASED A NEW RESIDENCE FOR HIS FAMILY, HE AVOIDED THE GRAND HOMES OF "THE HILL," WHERE THE LOCAL ELITE ARE SITUATED . . .

BUT CHOSE INSTEAD THE MODEST HOUSE ON LOWER SECOND STREET, CLOSE TO DOWN-TOWN AND HIS VARIED BUSINESS INTERESTS.

AVERSE TO MODERN CONVENIENCES, ANDREW SAW NEED FOR NEITHER GAS LIGHTING NOR INDOOR PLUMBING . . .

1ST FLOOR

2ND FLOOR

NOR FOR THE "WASTED SPACE" OF HALLWAYS: BOTH FLOORS HAD BEEN PARTITIONED INTO A MAZE OF INTERCONNECTING ROOMS.

WHEN I FIRST KNEW LIZZIE, SHE WAS ROBUST AND VIVACIOUS, POSSESSED OF A PLAYFUL AND GENEROUS NATURE.

SHE COULD CERTAINLY BE WILLFUL AND STUBBORN, BUT HER MORAL CHARACTER WAS ALWAYS OF THE HIGHEST ORDER. SHE MAINTAINED MEMBERSHIP IN THE CENTRAL CONGREGATIONAL CHURCH, WHERE SHE SOMETIMES TAUGHT IN THE SUNDAY-SCHOOL.

AS SHE MATURED, LIZZIE HAD HER SHARE OF ESCORTS AND SUITORS -- BUT NONE, TO MY KNOWLEDGE, EVER PRODUCED A SERIOUS OFFER.

LIKE MOST OF US, SHE WAS SUBJECT TO THE OCCASIONAL "SPELL" OR BLACK MOOD. FOR THESE, YOUNG LADIES HAD NO END OF REMEDIES FROM WHICH TO CHOOSE.

WHEN SHE TURNED THIRTY YEARS, LIZZIE WAS SENT ON A GRAND TOUR OF EUROPE WITH SEVERAL OTHER FALL RIVER LADIES. THEREAFTER, SHE SEEMED RESIGNED TO A LIFE OF SPINSTERHOOD.

SUCH SEEMED ALSO THE CASE WITH HER OLDER SISTER EMMA, WHOM I RECALL AS GENTLE-NATURED AND SHY TO THE POINT OF RECLUSIVENESS.

SHE HAD FEW FRIENDS AND WAS APPARENTLY CONTENT TO SPEND HER DAYS AT HOME.

IN LOOKS, LIZZIE FAVORED HER LATE MOTHER. — BUT SHE ALWAYS ENJOYED AN ESPECIAL BOND WITH HER FATHER.

TOGETHER THEY TOOK THE FISHING EXCURSIONS THAT WERE ANDREW'S ONLY PASTIME.

TO THE END OF HIS LIFE, HE WORE THE GOLDEN RING SHE HAD GIVEN HIM AS A GIRL.

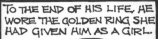

BUT I OFTEN WONDERED: HOW CLOSE A BOND COULD ONE ESTABLISH WITH SUCH A DISTANT AND FORBIDDING MAN?

THE FEELINGS OF BOTH DAUGHTERS TOWARD THEIR STEP-MOTHER HAVE LIKEWISE BEEN MUCH SPECULATED UPON.

ABBY'S ARRIVAL, SO SOON AFTER THE DEATH OF THEIR DEAR MOTHER, COULD NOT HAVE BEEN ENTIRELY PLEASANT.

TO MY RECOLLECTION, ABBY BORDEN WAS A PLAIN AND UNREMARKABLE SOUL — BETTER SUITED TO HER ROLE AS HOUSE-WIFE AND HELP-MEET THAN AS THE DEVIOUS MANIPULATOR THAT SOME HAVE PORTRAYED HER.

I KNOW THAT SOME RESENTMENT SURFACED IN 1887, WHEN ANDREW TRANSFERRED OWNERSHIP OF A HOUSE ON FOURTH STREET TO ABBY'S SISTER, MRS. SARAH WHITEHEAD.

COULD THE TWO DAUGHTERS, GETTING OLDER AND WITH NO PROSPECTS OF MARRIAGE, HAVE ENVISIONED THEIR INHERITANCE VANISHING PIECE-BY-PIECE INTO THE HANDS OF THEIR STEP-MOTHER'S FAMILY?

AN APPARENT BURGLARY IN 1891 MUST HAVE ADDED TO AN ATMOSPHERE OF MISTRUST.

CASH MONEY AND SEVERAL ITEMS OF JEWELRY WERE TAKEN FROM A BUREAU IN THE MASTER BEDROOM — EVIDENTLY BY A THIEF WHO KNEW JUST WHERE TO LOOK.

IT SEEMS TO HAVE BEEN AN OPEN SECRET WITHIN THE FAMILY THAT LIZZIE WAS THE CULPRIT.

(SHE HAD, AFTER ALL, BEEN ACCUSED YEARS EARLIER OF SHOP-LIFTING BY A NUMBER OF LOCAL MERCHANTS)

AFTER THIS INCIDENT, ANDREW BORDEN INITIATED THE PRACTICE OF LOCKING THE DOOR TO THE MASTER BEDROOM . . .

AND LEAVING THE KEY IN PLAIN VIEW ON THE MANTLE-PIECE IN THE SITTING ROOM.

THE CONNECTING DOOR BETWEEN THE MASTER BEDROOM AND THE REST OF THE SECOND FLOOR WAS SEALED OFF AS WELL.

RELATIONS BETWEEN ABBY AND BOTH HER STEP-DAUGHTERS APPEAR TO HAVE BECOME MINIMAL AND PERFUNCTORY. WHENEVER POSSIBLE, THEY TOOK THEIR MEALS SEPARATELY.

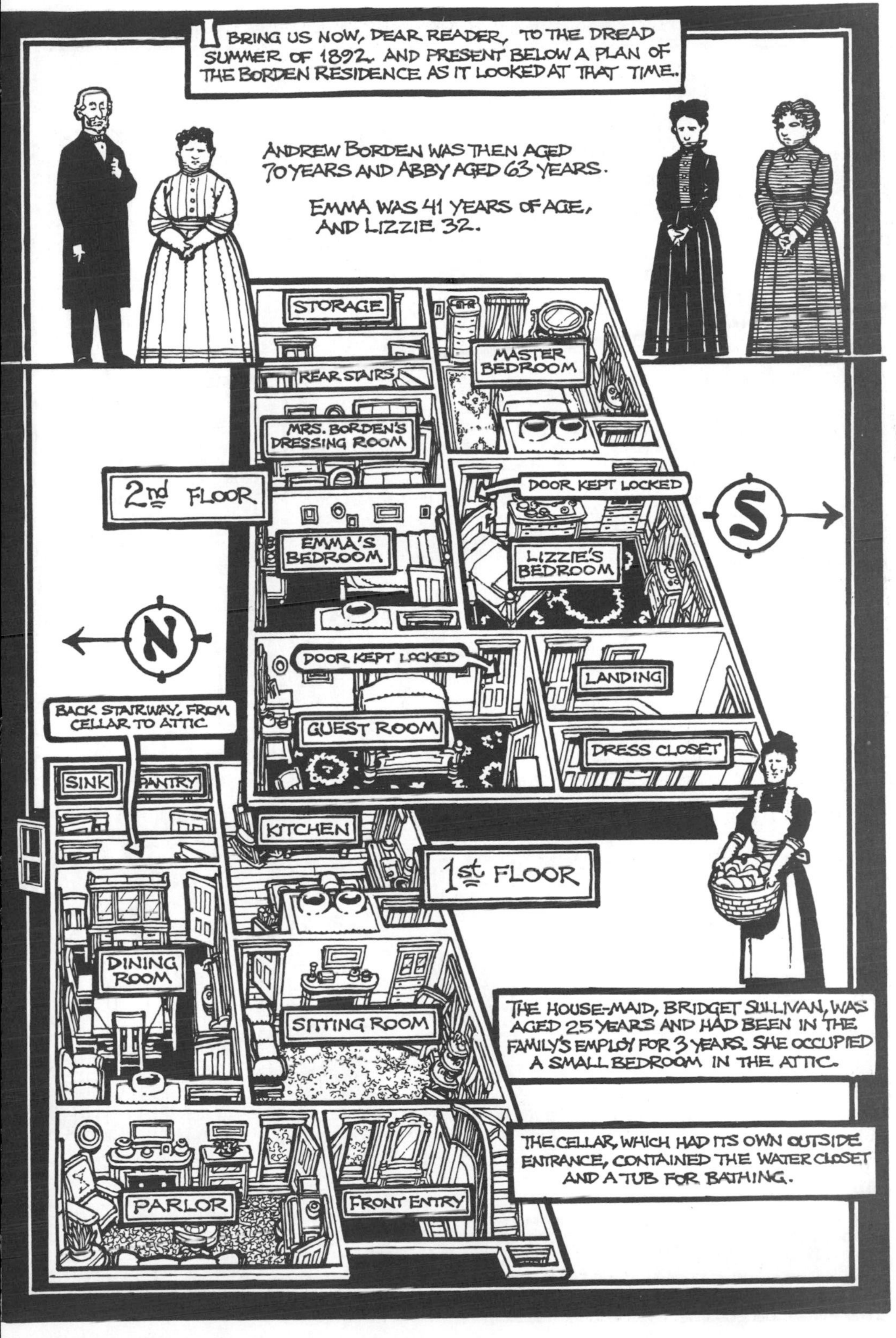
I BRING US NOW, DEAR READER, TO THE DREAD SUMMER OF 1892, AND PRESENT BELOW A PLAN OF THE BORDEN RESIDENCE AS IT LOOKED AT THAT TIME.
ANDREW BORDEN WAS THEN AGED 70 YEARS AND ABBY AGED 63 YEARS.
EMMA WAS 41 YEARS OF AGE, AND LIZZIE 32.
2nd FLOOR
STORAGE
REAR STAIRS
MRS. BORDEN'S DRESSING ROOM
MASTER BEDROOM
DOOR KEPT LOCKED
EMMA'S BEDROOM
LIZZIE'S BEDROOM
DOOR KEPT LOCKED
GUEST ROOM
LANDING
DRESS CLOSET
N
S
BACK STAIRWAY, FROM CELLAR TO ATTIC
SINK
PANTRY
KITCHEN
1st FLOOR
DINING ROOM
SITTING ROOM
PARLOR
FRONT ENTRY
THE HOUSE-MAID, BRIDGET SULLIVAN, WAS AGED 25 YEARS AND HAD BEEN IN THE FAMILY'S EMPLOY FOR 3 YEARS. SHE OCCUPIED A SMALL BEDROOM IN THE ATTIC.
THE CELLAR, WHICH HAD ITS OWN OUTSIDE ENTRANCE, CONTAINED THE WATER CLOSET AND A TUB FOR BATHING.

Sometime in May, there occurred an event that many people believe severed utterly the affections that Lizzie held for her father.

Lizzie, it must be remembered, was a fervent lover of all animals. She kept a roost in the loft of the barn for the wild pigeons of the neighborhood.

It seemed that, on two recent occasions, the barn had been broken into — no doubt by neighborhood boys hunting the birds.

And so, in an apparent effort to prevent further such intrusions, Andrew used a hatchet to behead every pigeon!

One is free to speculate upon how Lizzie, long accustomed by now to her father's various meannesses, was affected by this action.

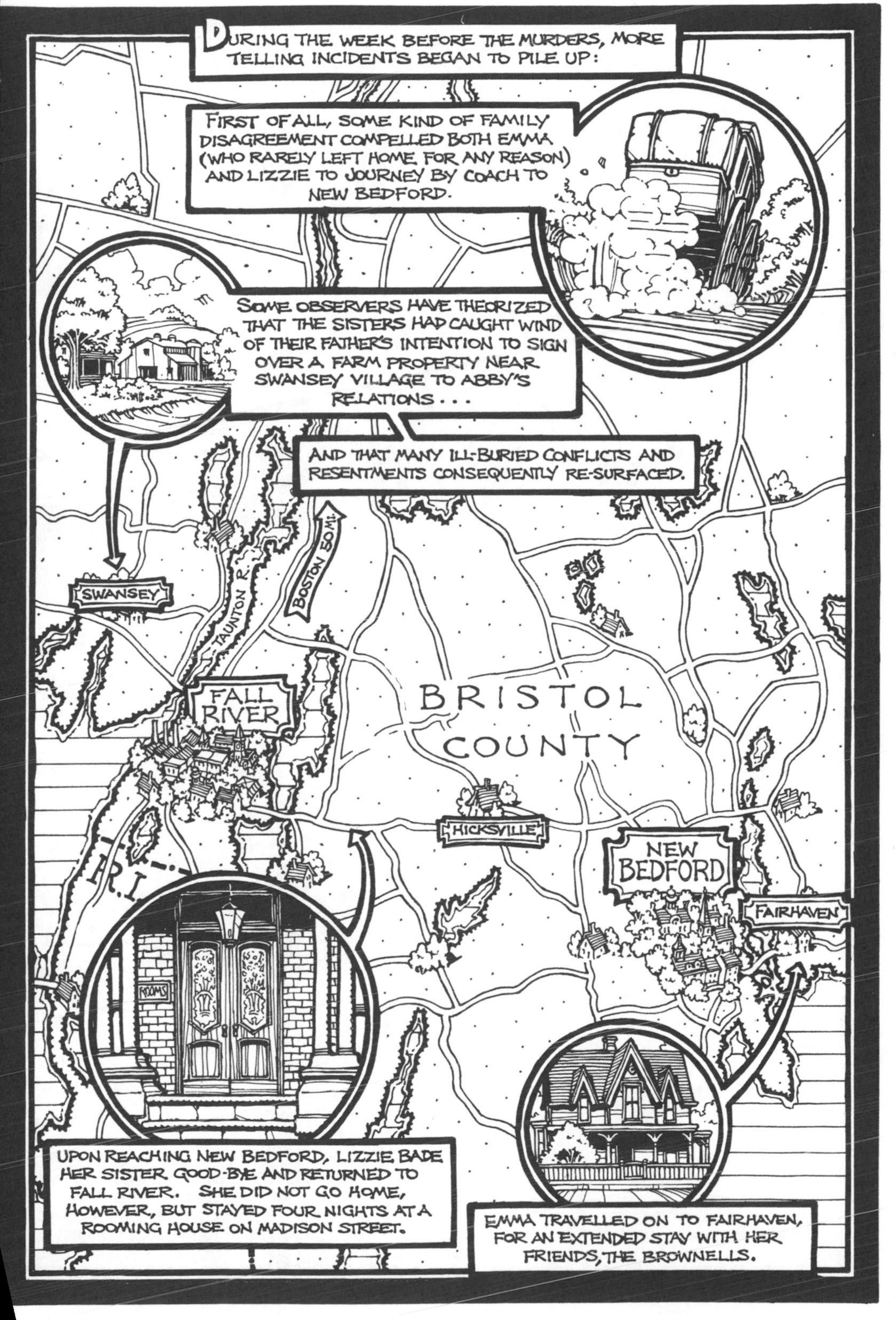
DURING THE WEEK BEFORE THE MURDERS, MORE TELLING INCIDENTS BEGAN TO PILE UP:
FIRST OF ALL, SOME KIND OF FAMILY DISAGREEMENT COMPELLED BOTH EMMA (WHO RARELY LEFT HOME FOR ANY REASON) AND LIZZIE TO JOURNEY BY COACH TO NEW BEDFORD.
SOME OBSERVERS HAVE THEORIZED THAT THE SISTERS HAD CAUGHT WIND OF THEIR FATHER'S INTENTION TO SIGN OVER A FARM PROPERTY NEAR SWANSEY VILLAGE TO ABBY'S RELATIONS . . .
AND THAT MANY ILL-BURIED CONFLICTS AND RESENTMENTS CONSEQUENTLY RE-SURFACED.
SWANSEY
TAUNTON R.
BOSTON 50 MI.
FALL RIVER
BRISTOL COUNTY
HICKSVILLE
NEW BEDFORD
FAIRHAVEN
R.I.
ROOMS
UPON REACHING NEW BEDFORD, LIZZIE BADE HER SISTER GOOD-BYE AND RETURNED TO FALL RIVER. SHE DID NOT GO HOME, HOWEVER, BUT STAYED FOUR NIGHTS AT A ROOMING HOUSE ON MADISON STREET.
EMMA TRAVELLED ON TO FAIRHAVEN, FOR AN EXTENDED STAY WITH HER FRIENDS, THE BROWNELLS.

TUESDAY, AUGUST 2 — TWO DAYS BEFORE THE TRAGEDY.

ⓞ ON THE MORNING AFTER LIZZIE'S RETURN HOME FROM HER STAY AT THE BOARDING HOUSE, BOTH ANDREW AND ABBY BORDEN AWOKE COMPLAINING OF STOMACH PAINS AND VOMITING IN THE NIGHT.

ABBY, IT SEEMED, HAD BEEN TAKEN WITH ESPECIAL VIOLENCE.

SHE WENT SO FAR AS TO WALK ACROSS THE STREET AND CALL UPON DR. SEABURY BOWEN, THE FAMILY'S FRIEND AND PHYSICIAN.

TO HIM, SHE CONFIDED HER SUSPICION THAT SHE AND HER HUSBAND HAD BEEN POISONED!

THE GOOD DOCTOR LISTENED SYMPATHETICALLY, BUT HE KNEW THAT SUCH STOMACH AILMENTS WERE NOT UNUSUAL DURING THE SUMMER MONTHS.

IN THOSE DAYS, AFTER ALL, FOOD PRESERVATION REMAINED IN A RATHER PRIMITIVE STATE. (A ROAST OF MUTTON, WHICH SUSTAINED THE FAMILY THROUGH SEVERAL MEALS THAT WEEK, WAS LATER ASSIGNED THE BLAME).

WEDNESDAY, AUGUST 3 — THE DAY BEFORE THE TRAGEDY.

ON THAT MORNING, A LADY (LATER IDENTIFIED BY SEVERAL WITNESSES AS LIZZIE BORDEN) ENTERED SMITH'S DRUG STORE ON SOUTH MAIN AT COLUMBIA STREET.

THIS ESTABLISHMENT, IT MUST BE NOTED, WAS FAR ENOUGH SOUTH ON MAIN ST. AS TO BE RARELY, IF EVER, PATRONIZED BY THE BORDENS OR ANYONE THEY KNEW.

THIS LADY ASKED TO PURCHASE PRUSSIC ACID — BUT THE PROPRIETOR, MR. ELI BENCE, REFUSED TO SELL HER THE DEADLY POISON WITHOUT A NOTE FROM A PHYSICIAN.

THE LADY PROTESTED INDIGNANTLY THAT SHE ONLY NEEDED "10 CENTS WORTH" TO CLEAN A SEALSKIN CAPE, THAT SHE NEVER HAD ANY TROUBLE OBTAINING IT BEFORE... AT LAST, SHE TURNED AND WALKED OUT. (LIZZIE LATER DENIED HAVING MADE THIS VISIT.)

THAT AFTERNOON, BY ANOTHER TRICK OF PROVIDENCE, JOHN V. MORSE, UNCLE TO THE BORDEN SISTERS, ARRIVED BY RAIL-CAR FROM HIS HOME IN NEW BEDFORD.

LITTLE IS KNOWN TODAY ABOUT THIS MAN — THEN AGED ABOUT 69 YEARS.

HE DRESSED SHABBILY, NEVER TOOK A WIFE. REPORTEDLY, HE HAD SPENT SEVERAL YEARS IN IOWA AS A HORSE TRADER.

UPON HIS RETURN TO THE EAST, HE AND ANDREW BECAME INVOLVED IN VARIOUS INVESTMENT SCHEMES — THUS NECESSITATING HIS INFREQUENT VISITS TO FALL RIVER.

AT ABOUT 7:00 PM THAT EVENING, LIZZIE PAID A CALL UPON MISS ALICE RUSSELL, A MAIDEN LADY WHO LIVED IN A SMALL HOUSE OFF OF THIRD STREET.

ALTHOUGH I KNEW HER ONLY SLIGHTLY, MISS RUSSELL HAD BEEN FOR YEARS THE CLOSEST OF FRIENDS TO BOTH EMMA AND LIZZIE.

AS MISS RUSSELL REMEMBERED IT, LIZZIE SEEMED NERVOUS THAT EVENING, AND OVERTAKEN BY A STRONG SENSE OF FOREBODING.

OH ALICE, I FEEL DEPRESSED — AS IF SOMETHING IS HANGING OVER ME — AND I CAN'T THROW IT OFF.

SHE RELATED THE FACTS OF HER FAMILY'S RECENT ILLNESS —

LAST NIGHT, FATHER AND ABBY WERE SO SICK... SOMETIMES I THINK OUR MILK MIGHT BE POISONED.

AND SHE TOLD OF HOW THE BORDEN HOUSE AND BARN HAD BEEN BROKEN INTO IN RECENT MONTHS.

I FEEL AFRAID THAT FATHER HAS AN ENEMY... HE HAS SO MUCH TROUBLE WITH THE MEN WHO COME TO SEE HIM.

THERE WAS ONE MAN WHO CAME BY. I DIDN'T SEE HIS FACE, BUT HE AND FATHER HAD A TERRIBLE ARGUMENT OVER SOME PROPERTY.

AS SHE PARTED FROM MISS RUSSELL, LIZZIE MADE A FINAL GRIM PREDICTION:

OH ALICE, I'M AFRAID SOMEBODY WILL DO SOMETHING! I DON'T KNOW BUT WHAT SOMEBODY WILL DO SOMETHING!

SHE ARRIVED HOME ABOUT 9:00 PM, TRIPLE-LOCKING THE FRONT DOOR, AS WAS THE FAMILY'S CUSTOM.

ANDREW AND ABBY AND JOHN MORSE TALKED IN THE SITTING ROOM AS LIZZIE, PAYING THEM NO GREETING, CLIMBED THE STAIRS TO HER BEDROOM.

SHE RECALLED LATER THAT, AS SHE PREPARED FOR BED, SHE COULD HEAR HER FATHER, UNCLE AND STEP-MOTHER IN LOUD, HEATED DISCUSSION BELOW . . .

BUT SHE COULD NOT MAKE OUT PRECISELY WHAT THEY WERE SAYING.

ONE FINAL INCIDENT SHOULD BE MENTIONED AT THIS POINT: AT ABOUT 11:00 PM, MRS. CHAGNON AND HER DAUGHTER, WHO OCCUPIED THE PROPERTY ADJACENT TO THE BORDEN BACK YARD, HEARD A DISTINCT AND SUSTAINED POUNDING — LASTING SOME FIVE MINUTES . . .

AND COMING FROM THE DIRECTION OF THE TALL WOODEN FENCE THAT SEPARATED THEIR PROPERTY FROM THE BORDENS'.

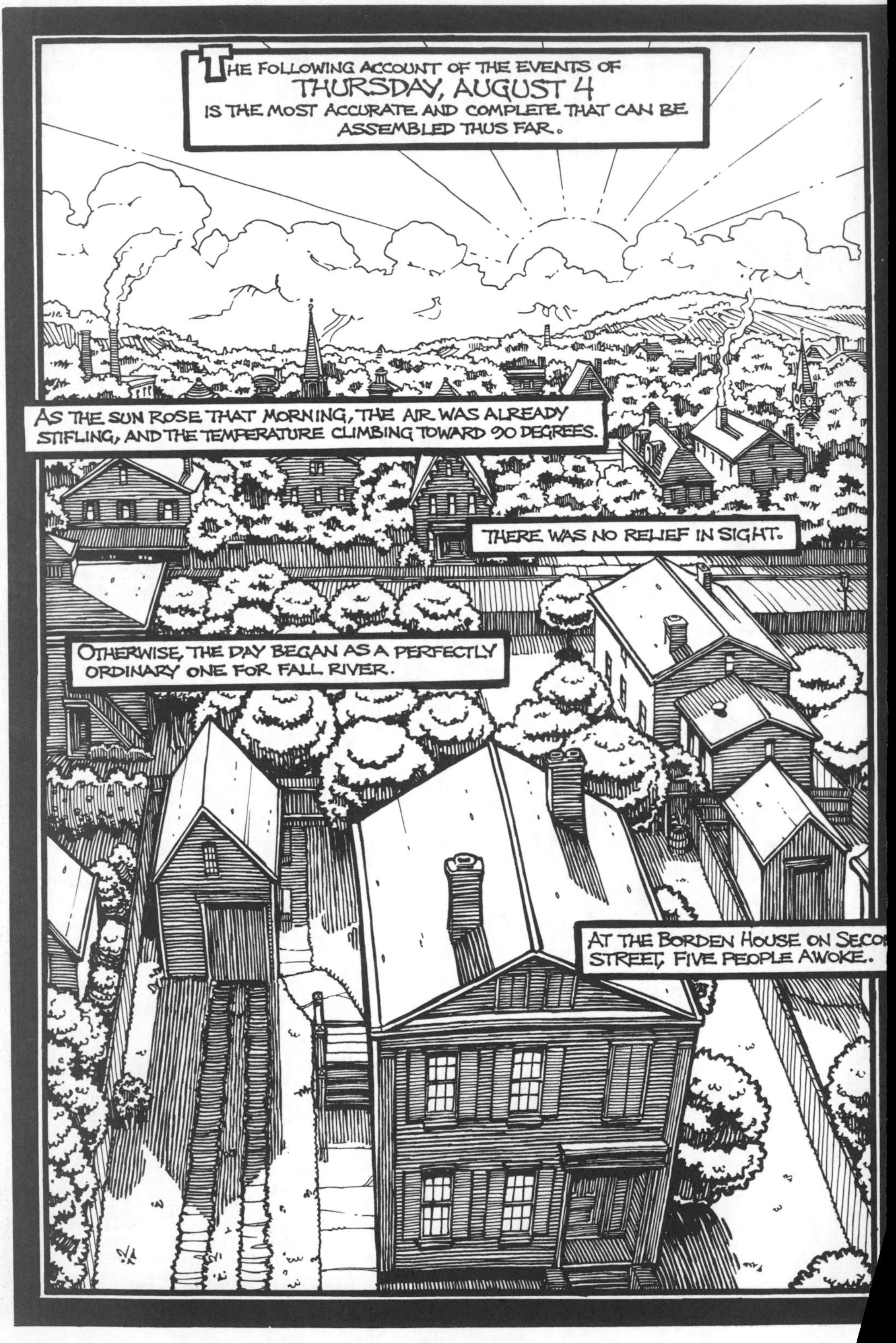
THE FOLLOWING ACCOUNT OF THE EVENTS OF
THURSDAY, AUGUST 4
IS THE MOST ACCURATE AND COMPLETE THAT CAN BE ASSEMBLED THUS FAR.
AS THE SUN ROSE THAT MORNING, THE AIR WAS ALREADY STIFLING, AND THE TEMPERATURE CLIMBING TOWARD 90 DEGREES.
THERE WAS NO RELIEF IN SIGHT.
OTHERWISE, THE DAY BEGAN AS A PERFECTLY ORDINARY ONE FOR FALL RIVER.
AT THE BORDEN HOUSE ON SECO
STREET, FIVE PEOPLE AWOKE.

SHORTLY AFTER 6:00 AM, JOHN V. MORSE, WHO SLEPT IN THE GUEST ROOM ON THE SECOND FLOOR, WAS DRESSED AND DOWNSTAIRS. HE OCCUPIED HIMSELF IN THE SITTING ROOM.

AT ABOUT THE SAME TIME, BRIDGET SULLIVAN AWOKE IN HER ATTIC ROOM. FEELING ILL AND DIZZY, SHE KNEW THAT THE FAMILY'S SICKNESS HAD CAUGHT UP TO HER.

WITH GREAT EFFORT, SHE TRUDGED DOWNSTAIRS, FIRST BRINGING COAL AND WOOD UP FROM THE CELLAR TO START THE KITCHEN FIRE.

AT ABOUT 6:30 AM, ABBY BORDEN CAME DOWN TO THE KITCHEN. THERE SHE GAVE BRIDGET HER INSTRUCTIONS FOR THE MORNING:

AFTER BREAKFAST, I WANT YOU TO WASH ALL THE DOWNSTAIRS WINDOWS, INSIDE AND OUT.

SHORTLY THEREAFTER, ANDREW BORDEN DESCENDED, LOOKING THE WORSE FOR HIS LINGERING ILLNESS.

HE EMPTIED HIS NIGHT-MUG IN THE BACK YARD BEFORE JOINING HIS WIFE AND JOHN MORSE IN THE SITTING ROOM.

AT ABOUT 7:00 AM, THE THREE SAT DOWN TO BREAKFAST. THE BILL OF FARE (WHICH HAS SINCE BECOME NOTORIOUS) CONSISTED OF: THE MUTTON ROAST (BY NOW SOME FIVE DAYS OLD) AND MUTTON BROTH, BREAD AND JOHNNY-CAKES, BANANAS, ORANGES, COOKIES AND COFFEE.

AFTER BREAKFAST, ANDREW AND JOHN RETIRED AGAIN TO THE SITTING ROOM...

WHILE ABBY BEGAN HER HOUSE-CLEANING CHORES DOWNSTAIRS.

WHILE CLEARING THE TABLE, BRIDGET SULLIVAN WAS SUDDENLY COMPELLED TO RUN INTO THE BACK YARD...

AND SPEND SEVERAL MINUTES AGAINST THE REAR FENCE RETCHING VIOLENTLY.

BY 8:45 AM, BRIDGET WAS BACK IN THE KITCHEN ...

AS JOHN MORSE LEFT THE HOUSE BY WAY OF THE REAR SCREEN DOOR. ANDREW SOON FOLLOWED.

THEY THEN STOOD OUTSIDE TALKING: JOHN WAS ON HIS WAY TO VISIT RELATIONS ACROSS TOWN AND INVITED ANDREW TO JOIN HIM.

ANDREW DECLINED, BUT INVITED JOHN BACK FOR THE NOON MEAL.

ANDREW THEN CAME BACK INSIDE, HOOKED THE SCREEN DOOR ...

AND CLIMBED THE REAR STAIRS TO HIS BEDROOM.

AT THIS TIME — ABOUT 9:00 AM — LIZZIE BORDEN CAME DOWN THE FRONT STAIRS. (EMMA BORDEN, THE READER WILL RECALL, WAS STILL WITH THE BROWNELLS AT FAIRHAVEN.)

WHAT WAS LIZZIE WEARING THAT MORNING? THE QUESTION HAS BECOME ONE OF INCREASING DISPUTE — BUT, FOR PRESENT PURPOSES, I WILL PLACE HER IN A LIGHT BLUE COTTON HOUSEDRESS.

AVOIDING THE MUTTON, SHE CONSUMED A LIGHT BREAKFAST OF COOKIES AND COFFEE.

AFTER SEVERAL MINUTES, ANDREW RETURNED DOWNSTAIRS, DRESSED IMMACULATELY AS ALWAYS — EVEN TO HIS PRINCE ALBERT COAT, DESPITE THE VICIOUS HEAT!

HE CONFERRED WITH ABBY ABOUT THE NOON MEAL; LIZZIE GAVE HIM SOME LETTERS TO POST FOR HER.

HE THEN LEFT, VIA THE REAR DOOR.

AT ABOUT 9:30 AM, ABBY CONTINUED HER HOUSECLEANING BY CLIMBING THE FRONT STAIRS TO THE GUEST ROOM...

WHILE BRIDGET SULLIVAN GRUDGINGLY WENT OUTDOORS TO BEGIN WASHING THE WINDOWS.

AND LIZZIE, HAVING FINISHED BREAKFAST, REMAINED IN THE DINING ROOM TO IRON SOME HANDKERCHIEFS.

THUS WAS THE STAGE SET FOR THE FIRST MURDER.

FOR NEARLY ONE HOUR, BRIDGET WORKED ON THE WINDOWS, BEGINNING ON THE SOUTH SIDE AND MOVING, IN TURN, TO THE WEST AND NORTH . . .

IT WAS AN ARDUOUS CHORE, WHICH NECESSITATED SEVERAL TRIPS TO THE PUMP IN THE BARN . . .

AT WHICH TASK SHE WAS SEEN BY SEVERAL PASSERS-BY ON SECOND STREET.

FROM WHICH VANTAGE POINT SHE WOULD PRESUMABLY HAVE NOTICED ANYBODY ENTERING OR LEAVING THE HOUSE.

BETWEEN TRIPS, SHE CHATTED OVER THE FENCE WITH THE MAID FROM THE KELLY HOUSE TO THE SOUTH.

AS SHE WORKED, BRIDGET COULD PEER INTO THE ROOMS OF THE FIRST FLOOR, WHERE SHE NOTED NO ACTIVITY AT ALL.

INSIDE THE HOUSE, LIZZIE'S MOVEMENTS ARE, OF COURSE, UNACCOUNTED FOR BY ANYBODY BUT HERSELF.

AS SHE LATER TOLD IT, ABBY WAS CALLED TO THE FRONT DOOR BY A MESSENGER WITH A NOTE.

THE NOTE, ABBY SAID, SUMMONED HER OUT TO VISIT A SICK FRIEND.

BUT WHETHER ABBY ACTUALLY LEFT, LIZZIE COULD NOT SAY, FOR SHE THEN WENT TO HER ROOM TO SORT SOME LAUNDRY.

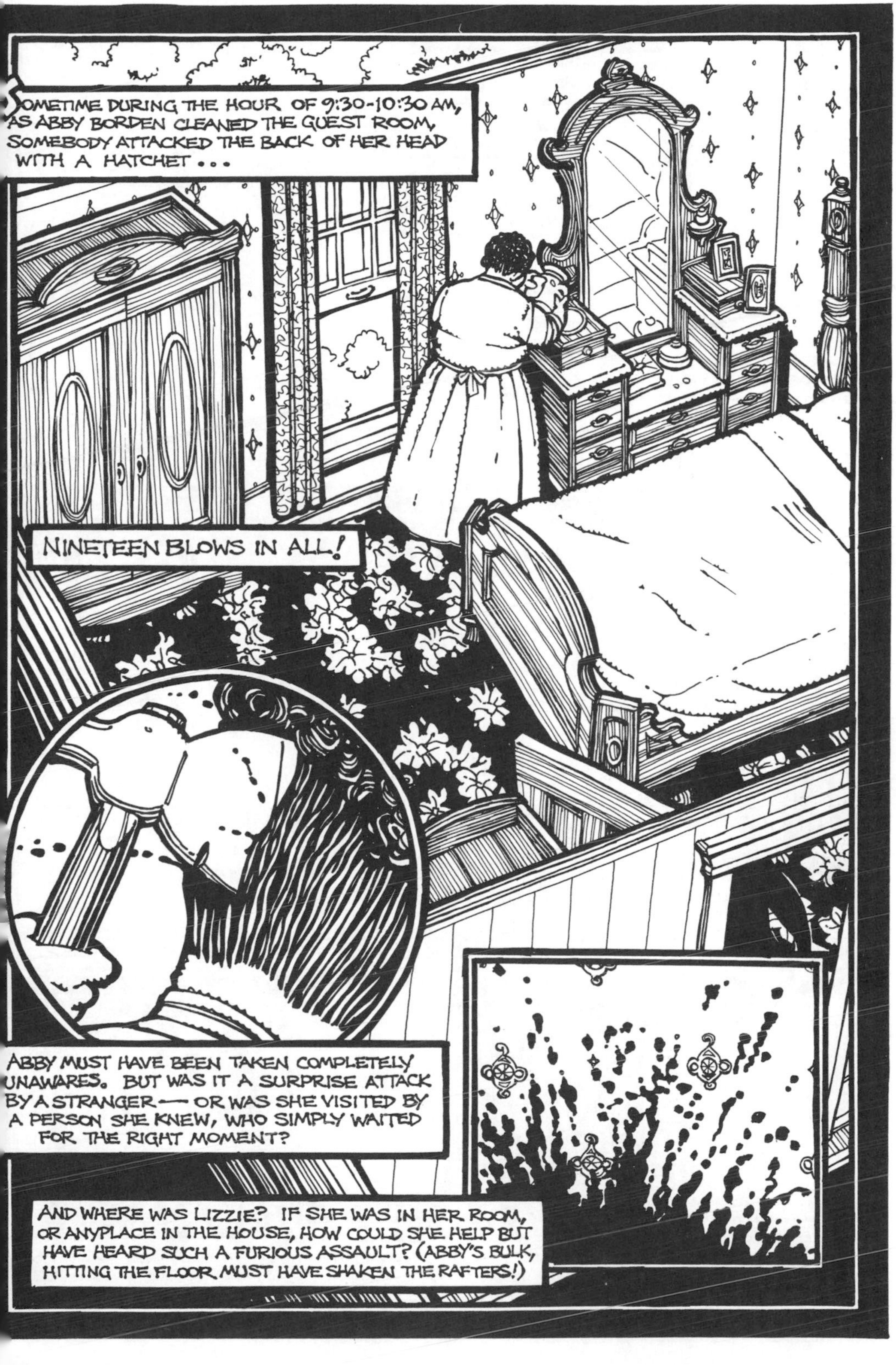
SOMETIME DURING THE HOUR OF 9:30-10:30 AM, AS ABBY BORDEN CLEANED THE GUEST ROOM, SOMEBODY ATTACKED THE BACK OF HER HEAD WITH A HATCHET . . .
NINETEEN BLOWS IN ALL!
ABBY MUST HAVE BEEN TAKEN COMPLETELY UNAWARES. BUT WAS IT A SURPRISE ATTACK BY A STRANGER — OR WAS SHE VISITED BY A PERSON SHE KNEW, WHO SIMPLY WAITED FOR THE RIGHT MOMENT?
AND WHERE WAS LIZZIE? IF SHE WAS IN HER ROOM, OR ANYPLACE IN THE HOUSE, HOW COULD SHE HELP BUT HAVE HEARD SUCH A FURIOUS ASSAULT? (ABBY'S BULK, HITTING THE FLOOR MUST HAVE SHAKEN THE RAFTERS!)

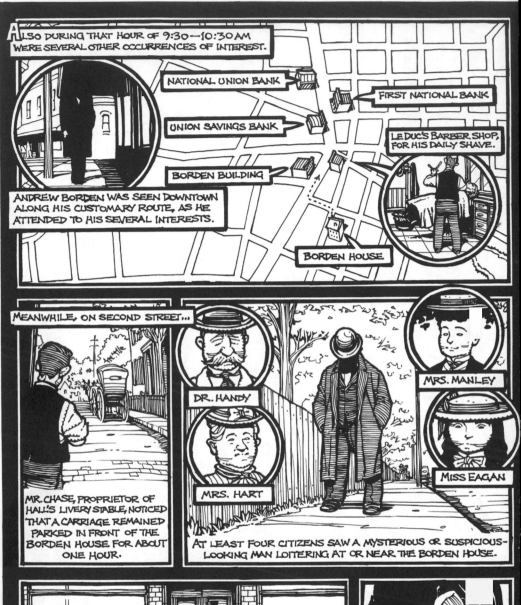

ALSO DURING THAT HOUR OF 9:30—10:30 AM WERE SEVERAL OTHER OCCURRENCES OF INTEREST.

NATIONAL UNION BANK

FIRST NATIONAL BANK

UNION SAVINGS BANK

LE DUC'S BARBER SHOP, FOR HIS DAILY SHAVE.

BORDEN BUILDING

ANDREW BORDEN WAS SEEN DOWNTOWN ALONG HIS CUSTOMARY ROUTE, AS HE ATTENDED TO HIS SEVERAL INTERESTS.

BORDEN HOUSE

MEANWHILE, ON SECOND STREET...

DR. HANDY

MRS. MANLEY

MRS. HART

MISS EAGAN

MR. CHASE, PROPRIETOR OF HALL'S LIVERY STABLE, NOTICED THAT A CARRIAGE REMAINED PARKED IN FRONT OF THE BORDEN HOUSE FOR ABOUT ONE HOUR.

AT LEAST FOUR CITIZENS SAW A MYSTERIOUS OR SUSPICIOUS-LOOKING MAN LOITERING AT OR NEAR THE BORDEN HOUSE.

AT ABOUT 10:45 AM, ANDREW CONCLUDED HIS FINAL MEETING— WITH A PROSPECTIVE TENNANT OF THE BORDEN BUILDING— AND BEGAN HIS WALK HOME.

MANY PEOPLE NOTICED THAT HE CARRIED A SMALL PARCEL UNDER HIS ARM.

AT ABOUT THIS SAME TIME, BRIDGET SULLIVAN CAME INDOORS TO WASH THE INTERIOR SIDE OF THE WINDOWS...

LOCKING THE SCREEN DOOR BEHIND HER.

SHORTLY THEREAFTER, ANDREW BORDEN ARRIVED HOME. HE FIRST TRIED THE REAR SCREEN DOOR...

AND THEN WALKED AROUND TO THE FRONT DOOR, WHICH WAS STILL TRIPLE-LOCKED FROM THE NIGHT BEFORE.

FINDING HE COULD NOT OPEN THE FRONT DOOR, HE KNOCKED HEAVILY UPON IT...

BRINGING BRIDGET FROM HER WORK.

AS THE MAID STRUGGLED WITH THE LOCKS, SHE UTTERED A MILD CURSE OF FRUSTRATION...

PSHAW!

UPON WHICH SHE HEARD A CURIOUS, MUTED LAUGH FROM THE DIRECTION OF THE UPSTAIRS LANDING.

KEE HEE!

SHE COULD NOT SEE FROM WHOM IT EMANATED, BUT ASSUMED IT TO HAVE BEEN LIZZIE.

AT LAST, ANDREW ENTERED THE HOUSE...

CARRYING, BRIDGET NOTICED, A SMALL WRAPPED PARCEL.

WHERE WAS LIZZIE WHEN HER FATHER ARRIVED HOME?

SHE LATER CLAIMED TO HAVE BEEN IN THE KITCHEN READING.

IN ANY CASE, SHE APPEARED IN THE DINING ROOM TO SPEAK BRIEFLY WITH HIM...

MENTIONING CASUALLY THAT ABBY HAD RECEIVED A MESSAGE AND GONE OUT.

AFTER SPENDING SOME MINUTES UPSTAIRS, ANDREW CAME DOWN TO THE SITTING ROOM.

AS HE RECLINED ON THE SOFA, LIZZIE CAME IN TO HELP HIM

DO YOU WANT THE WINDOW LEFT LIKE THIS?

SHE REMOVED HIS SHOES...

FOLDED HIS COAT UNDER HIS HEAD...

AND THE STAGE WAS SET FOR THE SECOND MURDER

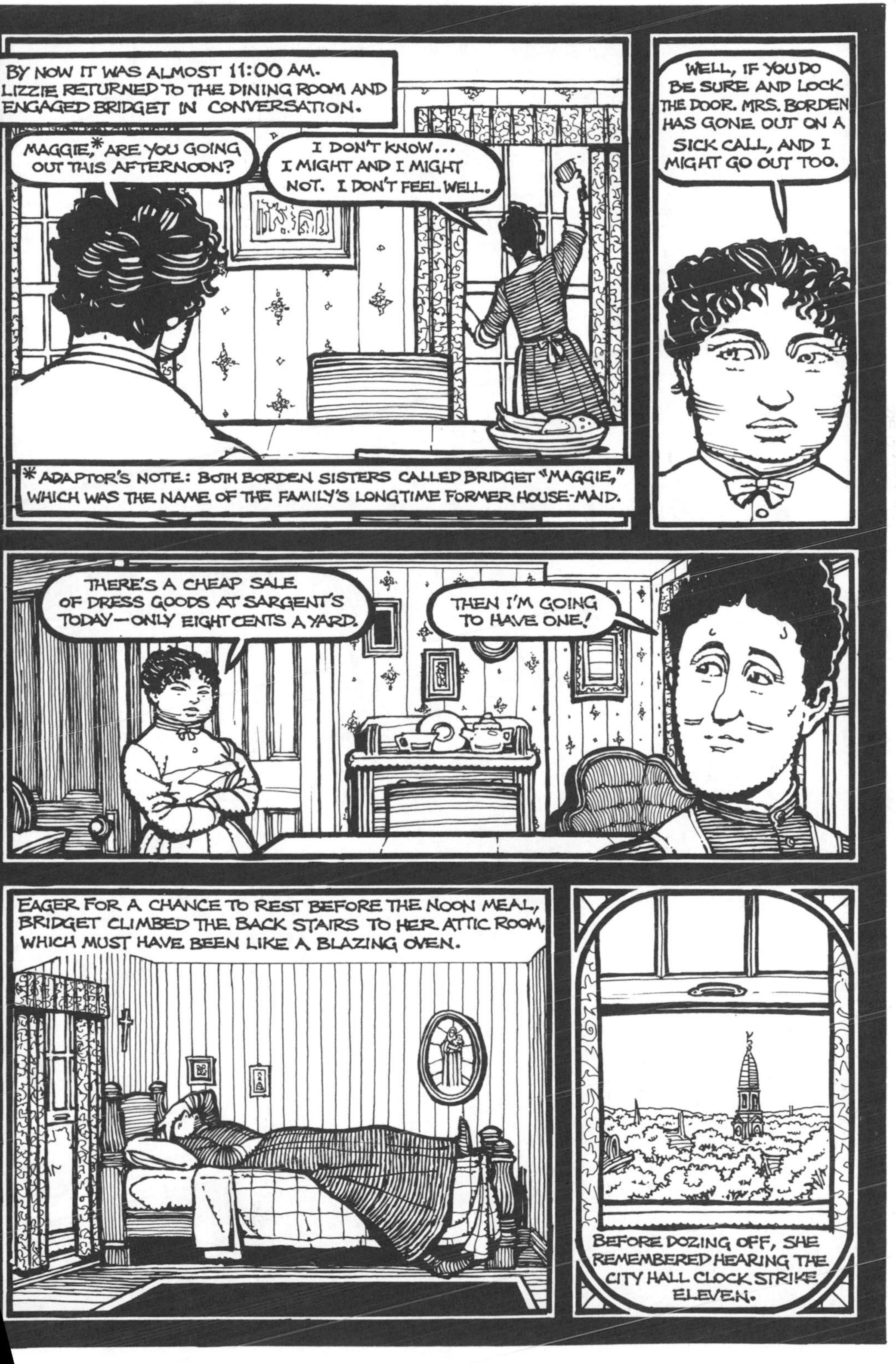
BY NOW IT WAS ALMOST 11:00 AM. LIZZIE RETURNED TO THE DINING ROOM AND ENGAGED BRIDGET IN CONVERSATION.
MAGGIE,* ARE YOU GOING OUT THIS AFTERNOON?
I DON'T KNOW... I MIGHT AND I MIGHT NOT. I DON'T FEEL WELL.
*ADAPTOR'S NOTE: BOTH BORDEN SISTERS CALLED BRIDGET "MAGGIE," WHICH WAS THE NAME OF THE FAMILY'S LONGTIME FORMER HOUSE-MAID.
WELL, IF YOU DO BE SURE AND LOCK THE DOOR. MRS. BORDEN HAS GONE OUT ON A SICK CALL, AND I MIGHT GO OUT TOO.
THERE'S A CHEAP SALE OF DRESS GOODS AT SARGENT'S TODAY—ONLY EIGHT CENTS A YARD.
THEN I'M GOING TO HAVE ONE!
EAGER FOR A CHANCE TO REST BEFORE THE NOON MEAL, BRIDGET CLIMBED THE BACK STAIRS TO HER ATTIC ROOM, WHICH MUST HAVE BEEN LIKE A BLAZING OVEN.
BEFORE DOZING OFF, SHE REMEMBERED HEARING THE CITY HALL CLOCK STRIKE ELEVEN.

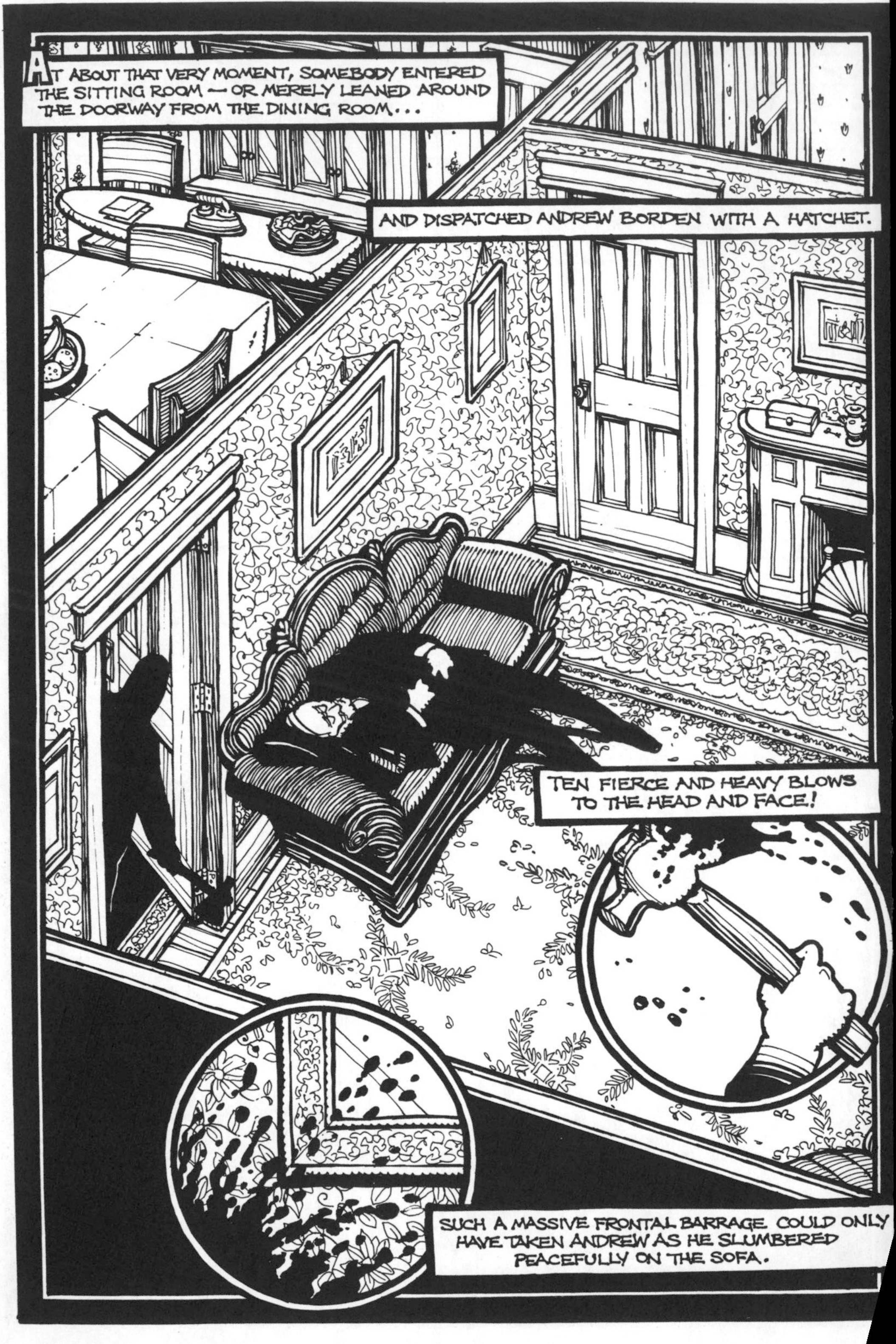
AT ABOUT THAT VERY MOMENT, SOMEBODY ENTERED THE SITTING ROOM — OR MERELY LEANED AROUND THE DOORWAY FROM THE DINING ROOM...
AND DISPATCHED ANDREW BORDEN WITH A HATCHET.
TEN FIERCE AND HEAVY BLOWS TO THE HEAD AND FACE!
SUCH A MASSIVE FRONTAL BARRAGE COULD ONLY HAVE TAKEN ANDREW AS HE SLUMBERED PEACEFULLY ON THE SOFA.

WHERE WAS LIZZIE AT THE TIME HER FATHER WAS MURDERED? SHE CLAIMED, THEN AND EVER AFTER, THAT SHE WAS OUTSIDE THE HOUSE.

A PASSING ICE CREAM VENDOR, MR. LUBINSKY, SAW A WOMAN IN THE BORDEN YARD AT ABOUT THAT VERY TIME.

WHEN SHE CAME BACK INSIDE — VIA THE REAR SCREEN DOOR — SHE PASSED THROUGH THE SITTING ROOM ON THE WAY TO THE FRONT STAIRS.

GLANCING TO HER LEFT, SHE DISCOVERED THE GRISLY REMAINS OF HER FATHER.

BRIDGET WAS JOLTED AWAKE BY LIZZIE'S CRIES.

MAGGIE, COME DOWN!

COME QUICK! FATHER'S DEAD! SOMEBODY KILLED HIM!

BRIDGET CAME DOWNSTAIRS TO CONFRONT LIZZIE IN THE REAR HALLWAY.

HE'S IN THE SITTING ROOM, BUT DON'T LOOK. GO FIND DR. BOWEN.

AS SHE DASHED FROM THE HOUSE, BRIDGET NOTED THAT THE SCREEN DOOR HAD BEEN UNHOOKED.

FINDING THE DOCTOR OUT (AND LEAVING AN URGENT MESSAGE WITH MRS. BOWEN) BRIDGET RETURNED TO THE REAR DOOR.

WHAT HAPPENED, MISS? DID YOU SEE?

NO—I WAS OUT IN THE YARD. I HEARD A GROAN AND CAME IN. NOW GO FETCH MISS RUSSELL.

MRS. ADELAIDE CHURCHILL, A WIDOW WHO OCCUPIED THE HOUSE NORTH OF THE BORDENS, HAD BEEN WATCHING THE ACTIVITY NEXT DOOR. SHE WALKED OVER AS BRIDGET DEPARTED AGAIN.

LIZZIE, WHAT'S THE MATTER?

TO HER, LIZZIE APPEARED DAZED AND STUNNED.

OH, MRS. CHURCHILL... SOMEONE HAS KILLED FATHER.

MRS. CHURCHILL BROUGHT LIZZIE INTO THE KITCHEN AND SAT HER IN THE ROCKER THERE.

AND THEN PEERED INTO THE SITTING ROOM TO CONFIRM THE HORRIBLE TALE.

TO MRS. CHURCHILL'S INQUIRIES, LIZZIE REPLIED: THAT SHE HAD BEEN OUT IN THE BARN, LOOKING FOR "IRONS," AND HAD HEARD NOISES COMING FROM THE HOUSE...

AND NO, ABBY WAS NOT AT HOME, HAVING RECEIVED A MESSAGE AND GONE OUT.

AT THIS POINT, IT MUST BE MENTIONED THAT MRS. CHURCHILL — WHO ARRIVED NO MORE THAN TEN MINUTES AFTER ANDREW'S MURDER — SAW NO BLOOD ON LIZZIE'S DRESS, SKIN OR HAIR, AND HER HAIR NEATLY PINNED UP, WITH NO SIGN OF HAVING BEEN RECENTLY WASHED.

MRS. CHURCHILL THEN LEFT LIZZIE ALONE AND WALKED DOWN SECOND STREET TO HALL'S LIVERY STABLE.

THERE, SHE FOUND HER HIRED MAN AND ORDERED HIM TO GO FIND A DOCTOR. THERE HAD BEEN "TROUBLE" AT THE BORDEN HOUSE.

SHE ALSO SUGGESTED THAT SOMEBODY TELEPHONE THE POLICE.

THIS WAS AT 11:15 AM.

DR. BOWEN ARRIVED, WITH MRS. BOWEN . . .

BRIDGET SULLIVAN RETURNED FROM MISS RUSSELL'S HOUSE . . .

AND, SHORTLY THEREAFTER, MISS RUSSELL HERSELF ARRIVED.

THE DOCTOR, AFTER SATISFYING HIMSELF AS TO ANDREW BORDEN'S DECEASE, CALLED FOR A SHEET TO PLACE OVER THE BODY . . .

WHILE, IN THE KITCHEN, THE WOMEN ATTEMPTED TO COMFORT LIZZIE. WHEN MISS RUSSELL REACHED TO LOOSEN HER COLLAR, LIZZIE STOPPED HER.

I'M NOT FAINT.

AT THAT POINT, DR. BOWEN REMOVED LIZZIE TO A SMALL DIVAN IN THE DINING ROOM.

SHE TOLD HIM THAT SHE HAD BEEN OUT IN THE BARN, "LOOKING FOR IRONS" WHEN HER FATHER WAS KILLED.

SHE THEN SENT THE DOCTOR OUT TO TELEGRAPH THE TERRIBLE NEWS TO EMMA IN FAIRHAVEN . . .

PERHAPS ALSO TO NOTIFY JOHN MORSE AT THE HOME OF HIS RELATIONS ON WEYBOSSET STREET.

AS DR. BOWEN LEFT ON HIS MISSION, THE FIRST POLICE OFFICER ARRIVED.

THIS WAS OFFICER GEORGE ALLEN, WHO WAS THE ONLY MAN ON DUTY AT THE STATION...

(BECAUSE, ON THAT VERY DAY, MOST OF THE FALL RIVER POLICE FORCE WERE ON THEIR ANNUAL OUTING TO ROCKY POINT!)

HE TOOK A LOOK AT THE CORPSE...

SEARCHED THE FIRST FLOOR FOR ANY LURKING INTRUDER (ALTHOUGH NOT THE SECOND FLOOR OR THE CELLAR)...

AND DEPARTED TO LOCATE MORE OFFICERS, LEAVING A BURLY CITIZEN, MR. CHARLES SAWYER, TO GUARD THE DOOR.

IN THE DINING ROOM, MEANWHILE, MRS. CHURCHILL WONDERED AGAIN ABOUT ABBY BORDEN'S WHEREABOUTS. LIZZIE REPLIED OFFHANDEDLY:

I THOUGHT I HEARD HER COME IN THE FRONT DOOR.

AND SO, WITH DREAD IN THEIR HEARTS, MRS. CHURCHILL AND BRIDGET SULLIVAN ASCENDED THE FRONT STAIRS.

LOOKING INTO THE GUEST ROOM AT FLOOR LEVEL, MRS. CHURCHILL KNEW AT ONCE WHAT SHE SAW...

THE BUTCHERED REMAINS OF ABBY BORDEN!

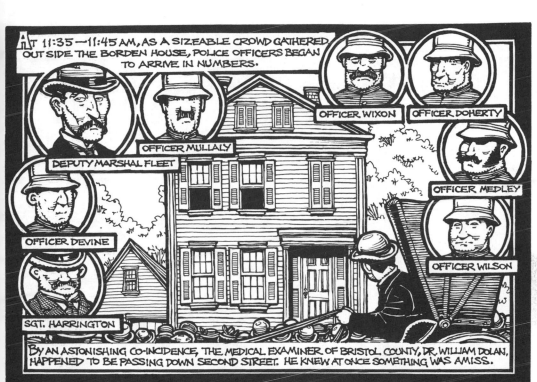

AT 11:35 — 11:45 AM, AS A SIZEABLE CROWD GATHERED OUTSIDE THE BORDEN HOUSE, POLICE OFFICERS BEGAN TO ARRIVE IN NUMBERS.

DEPUTY MARSHAL FLEET

OFFICER MULLALY

OFFICER WIXON

OFFICER DOHERTY

OFFICER MEDLEY

OFFICER DEVINE

OFFICER WILSON

SGT. HARRINGTON

BY AN ASTONISHING CO-INCIDENCE, THE MEDICAL EXAMINER OF BRISTOL COUNTY, DR. WILLIAM DOLAN, HAPPENED TO BE PASSING DOWN SECOND STREET. HE KNEW AT ONCE SOMETHING WAS AMISS.

THE POLICE INITIATED A THOROUGH SEARCH OF THE HOUSE...

WHILE LIZZIE, IN HER FIRST OFFICIAL INTERVIEW, (FROM OFFICER MEDLEY), TOLD OF HER TRIP TO THE BARN DURING THE TIME HER FATHER WAS KILLED. SHE CLIMBED TO THE LOFT, SHE SAID, IN SEARCH OF IRON PIECES TO USE AS SINKERS FOR AN UPCOMING FISHING EXCURSION.

SHE FIGURED SHE WAS THERE FOR FIFTEEN OR TWENTY MINUTES.

IN THE MEAN-TIME, JOHN V. MORSE, HAVING RETURNED BY STREET-CAR, APPROACHED THE HOUSE CAUTIOUSLY.

SEVERAL PEOPLE SAW HIM LOITERING AT THE SIDE OF THE HOUSE AND IN THE BACK YARD BEFORE HE FINALLY ENTERED.

As many as two dozen officers swarmed over the house and grounds. No sign of breaking and entering could be found, nor any evidence of a struggle or robbery.

The front door remained securely locked . . . as did the rear door leading to the cellar.

No drops of blood were found outside the house — nor in any other room save those in which the victims lay.

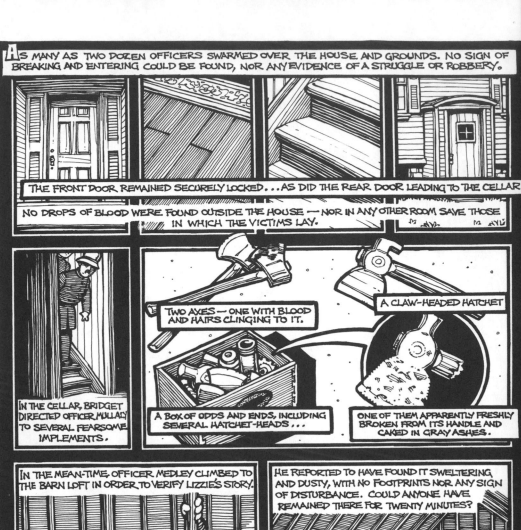

In the cellar, Bridget directed Officer Mullaly to several fearsome implements.

Two axes — one with blood and hairs clinging to it.

A box of odds and ends, including several hatchet-heads . . .

A claw-headed hatchet

One of them apparently freshly broken from its handle and caked in gray ashes.

In the mean-time, Officer Medley climbed to the barn loft in order to verify Lizzie's story.

He reported to have found it sweltering and dusty, with no footprints nor any sign of disturbance. Could anyone have remained there for twenty minutes?

Officer Wixon climbed a lumber pile at the rear fence and vaulted onto the Chagnon property behind the Bordens.

Workers there reported having seen or heard nothing unusual all morning.

THE MEDICAL EXAMINER, AFTER A PRELIMINARY SCRUTINY OF THE BODIES, ANNOUNCED TWO IMMEDIATE CONCLUSIONS:

MRS. BORDEN WAS KILLED SOME TIME BEFORE HER HUSBAND — PERHAPS TWO HOURS!

(IF SO, COULD A MURDERER HAVE HIDDEN WITHIN THE HOUSE FOR THAT LENGTH OF TIME — OR DEPARTED AND RETURNED WITHOUT BEING SEEN?)

EACH ATTACK WAS OF SUCH FEROCITY THAT THE FIRST BLOW WAS SUFFICIENT TO CAUSE DEATH.

(IN OTHER WORDS, THIS WAS THE PRODUCT OF NO COMMONPLACE FELONY — BUT THE KIND OF OVER-KILL THAT MARKS THE WORK OF A HOPELESS MANIAC.)

THE POLICE PHOTOGRAPHER ARRIVED TO CAPTURE IMAGES OF THE TWO VICTIMS, AS THEY LAY WHERE THEY WERE FOUND.

THE PHOTOGRAPHS BECAME THE TALK OF FALL RIVER.

IT WAS BRUTAL MID-AFTERNOON WHEN THE BODIES WERE AT LAST BROUGHT INTO THE DINING ROOM, LAID OUT UPON THE TABLE, STRIPPED AND WASHED. DR. DOLAN, ASSISTED BY DR. BOWEN AND FIVE OTHER PHYSICIANS PERFORMED THE POST-MORTEM.

TOWNSPEOPLE JOCKEYED FOR A VIEW THROUGH THE WIDE-OPEN WINDOWS...

WHILE COUNTLESS FLIES, ATTRACTED BY THE BLOOD, FILLED THE STIFLING AIR WITHIN THE HOUSE.

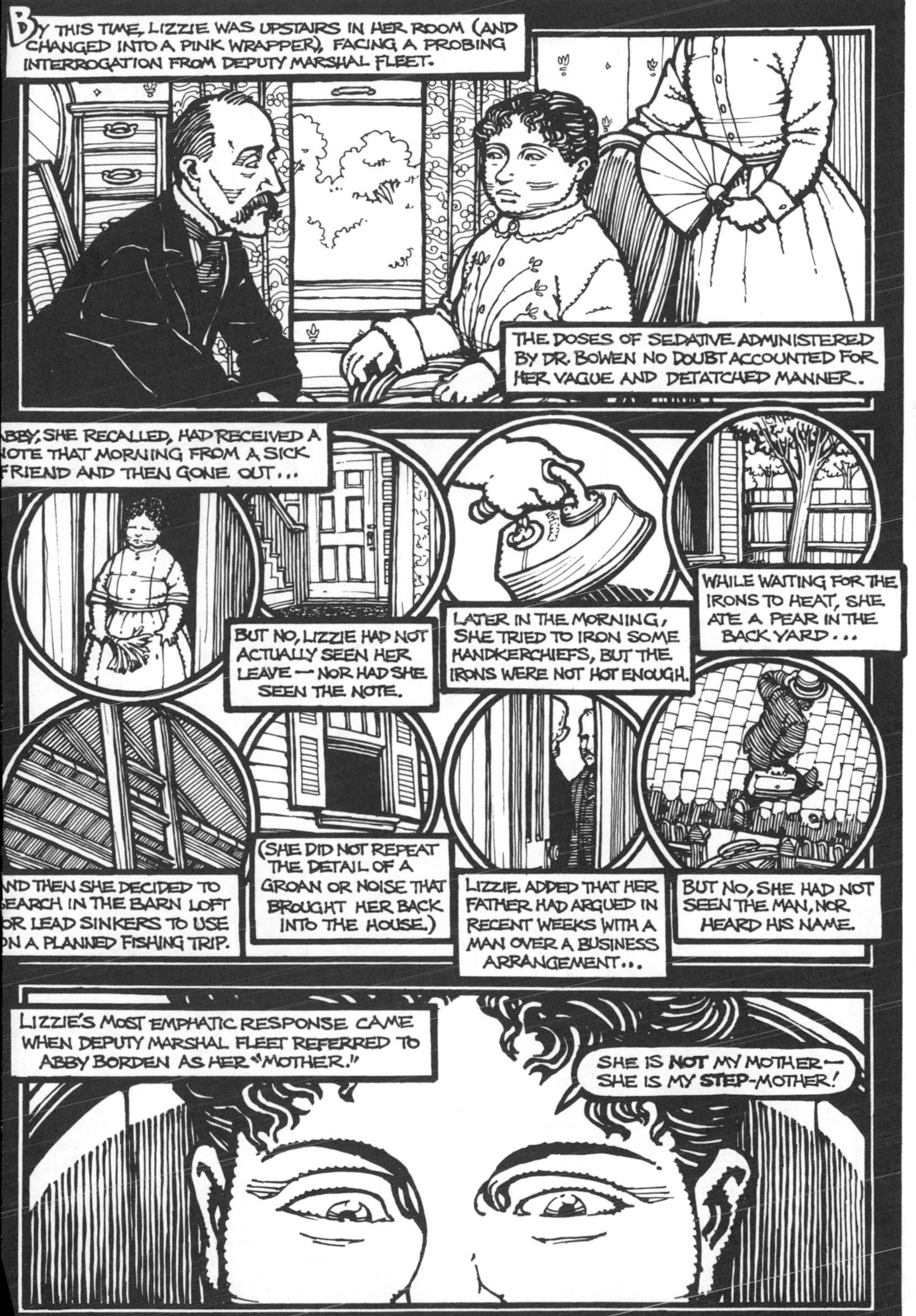
BY THIS TIME, LIZZIE WAS UPSTAIRS IN HER ROOM (AND CHANGED INTO A PINK WRAPPER), FACING A PROBING INTERROGATION FROM DEPUTY MARSHAL FLEET.
THE DOSES OF SEDATIVE ADMINISTERED BY DR. BOWEN NO DOUBT ACCOUNTED FOR HER VAGUE AND DETATCHED MANNER.
ABBY, SHE RECALLED, HAD RECEIVED A NOTE THAT MORNING FROM A SICK FRIEND AND THEN GONE OUT...
BUT NO, LIZZIE HAD NOT ACTUALLY SEEN HER LEAVE — NOR HAD SHE SEEN THE NOTE.
LATER IN THE MORNING, SHE TRIED TO IRON SOME HANDKERCHIEFS, BUT THE IRONS WERE NOT HOT ENOUGH.
WHILE WAITING FOR THE IRONS TO HEAT, SHE ATE A PEAR IN THE BACK YARD...
AND THEN SHE DECIDED TO SEARCH IN THE BARN LOFT FOR LEAD SINKERS TO USE ON A PLANNED FISHING TRIP.
(SHE DID NOT REPEAT THE DETAIL OF A GROAN OR NOISE THAT BROUGHT HER BACK INTO THE HOUSE.)
LIZZIE ADDED THAT HER FATHER HAD ARGUED IN RECENT WEEKS WITH A MAN OVER A BUSINESS ARRANGEMENT...
BUT NO, SHE HAD NOT SEEN THE MAN, NOR HEARD HIS NAME.
LIZZIE'S MOST EMPHATIC RESPONSE CAME WHEN DEPUTY MARSHAL FLEET REFERRED TO ABBY BORDEN AS HER "MOTHER."
SHE IS NOT MY MOTHER — SHE IS MY STEP-MOTHER!

AT 7:00 PM, EMMA BORDEN ARRIVED FROM FAIRHAVEN

THE SISTERS' REUNION TOOK PLACE IN THE PARLOR...

AS THE HOUSE UNDERWENT ANOTHER TOP-TO-BOTTOM SEARCH:

ESPECIAL ATTENTION WAS PAID TO BUREAUS AND CLOSETS, IN SEARCH OF BLOOD-SPATTERED CLOTHING.

A GREAT EFFORT WAS MADE TO FIND THE NOTE THAT LIZZIE SAID HER STEP-MOTHER HAD RECEIVED.

IT MUST BE MENTIONED, HOWEVER, THAT NO SUCH NOTE WAS EVER FOUND, NOR ANY MESSENGER OR SICK FRIEND OF ABBY'S.

THE FIREPLACES AND ASH-BINS WERE SIFTED FOR TRACES OF THE MURDER WEAPON.

THAT EVENING, IN THE KITCHEN, SGT. HARRINGTON WATCHED DR BOWEN RIP SEVERAL PAGES FROM HIS NOTE-BOOK AND DROP THEM INTO THE FIRE.

THE CROWD OUTSIDE THE BORDEN HOUSE DIMINISHED ONLY SLIGHTLY WHEN DARKNESS FELL.

AS POLICE OFFICERS STOOD WATCH DOWNSTAIRS, EMMA AND LIZZIE RETIRED TO THEIR BEDROOMS.

JOHN V. MORSE AGAIN OCCUPIED THE GUEST ROOM . . .

AND MISS ALICE RUSSELL BEGAN AN EXTENDED STAY IN THE MASTER BEDROOM.

ONLY BRIDGET SULLIVAN REFUSED TO SPEND ANOTHER NIGHT IN THE HOUSE. SHE FOUND QUARTERS IN THE HOME OF A NEIGHBOR.

COULD ANY OF THEM HAVE SLUMBERED PEACEFULLY THAT NIGHT?

ANDREW AND ABBY BORDEN REMAINED UPON THE TABLE FROM WHICH THEY HAD CONSUMED BREAKFAST THAT VERY MORNING!

FOR THE ENTIRETY OF FRIDAY, AUGUST 5, THE BORDEN SISTERS STAYED INDOORS, AS REPORTS OF THE GRUESOME DOUBLE MURDER SPREAD ACROSS THE NATION AND THE WORLD.

THE CURIOUS KEPT THEIR VIGIL OUTSIDE, WHILE POLICE SUBJECTED THE HOUSE TO YET ANOTHER THOROUGH SEARCH.

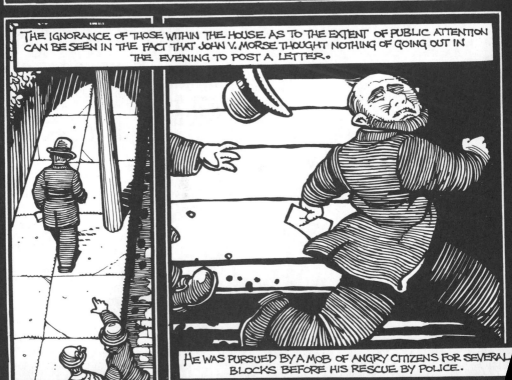

THE IGNORANCE OF THOSE WITHIN THE HOUSE AS TO THE EXTENT OF PUBLIC ATTENTION CAN BE SEEN IN THE FACT THAT JOHN V. MORSE THOUGHT NOTHING OF GOING OUT IN THE EVENING TO POST A LETTER.

HE WAS PURSUED BY A MOB OF ANGRY CITIZENS FOR SEVERAL BLOCKS BEFORE HIS RESCUE BY POLICE.

THE MORNING OF **SATURDAY, AUGUST 6** SAW AN EDITORIAL IN THE FALL RIVER GLOBE, CHIDING THE POLICE FORCE FOR ITS INACTION THUS FAR.

EVERYBODY WONDERED WHEN AN ARREST WOULD BE MADE.

AT 10:00 AM, A SMALL, PRIVATE FUNERAL SERVICE WAS HELD AT THE BORDEN HOUSE.

THE CASKETS WERE DISPLAYED IN THE SITTING ROOM.

AFTERWARD, A PARADE OF CARRIAGES FOLLOWED THE TWIN HEARSES TO OAK GROVE CEMETERY.

THRONGS OF CITIZENS LINED THE ROUTE.

BUT MR. AND MRS. BORDEN WERE STILL FAR FROM THEIR FINAL REST...

AFTER A BRIEF GRAVESIDE SERVICE, THE BODIES WERE RECLAIMED BY THE AUTHORITIES ...

AND REMOVED TO AN EMPTY TOMB FOR FURTHER EXAMINATION!

AT ABOUT THAT SAME MOMENT, CITY MARSHAL RUFUS HILLIARD, IN FRUSTRATION, CONDUCTED ANOTHER SEARCH OF THE BORDEN HOUSE...

DOWN TO THE SLIGHTEST BUMP IN THE WALLPAPER!

HE TOOK WITH HIM THE BLUE COTTON-AND-SILK DRESS THAT LIZZIE CLAIMED TO HAVE WORN ON THE MORNING OF THE MURD

THAT EVENING, MARSHAL HILLIARD RETURNED WITH MR. JOHN COUGHLIN, THE MAYOR OF FALL RIVER. EVERYBODY GATHERED IN THE PARLOR.

WHEN THE MAYOR SUGGESTED THAT THE FAMILY REMAIN INDOORS FOR THE NEXT SEVERAL DAYS, LIZZIE CHALLENGED HIM:

WHY? IS ANYBODY IN THIS HOUSE SUSPECTED?

IN VIEW OF WHAT HAPPENED TO MR. MORSE LAST NIGHT, THE INFERENCE MIGHT BE JUSTIFIED.

LIZZIE WOULD NOT BACK DOWN.

I WANT TO KNOW THE TRUTH! IS ANYBODY SUSPECTED?

WELL, MISS BORDEN, I REGRET TO ANSWER ... BUT YES, YOU ARE SUSPECTED.

LIZZIE CALMLY ROSE AND EXTENDED HER WRISTS.

I AM READY TO GO NOW.

THE MAYOR AND MARSHAL HILLIARD HASTENED TO ASSURE HER THAT SHE WAS NOT UNDER ARREST, AND THAT THEIR CONCERN WAS ONLY FOR THE FAMILY'S SAFETY.

AND THEN THEY POLITELY TOOK THEIR LEAVE

ON SUNDAY, AUGUST 7, THERE OCCURRED AN INCIDENT THAT WAS TO REFLECT BADLY UPON LIZZIE IN THE MONTHS TO COME. ON THAT MORNING, SHE AND EMMA WORKED IN THE KITCHEN.

WHAT ARE YOU GOING TO DO WITH THAT?

I'M GOING TO BURN THIS OLD THING UP. IT'S COVERED WITH PAINT.

AND SO, SHE BEGAN TO DROP PIECES OF A BLUE CORDUROY DRESS INTO THE FLAMES.

AT THIS POINT, MISS ALICE RUSSELL, STILL STAYING WITH THE SISTERS, ENTERED THE ROOM.

LIZZIE, WHAT ARE YOU DOING?

JUST BURNING UP THIS OLD DRESS.

I WOULDN'T LET ANYBODY SEE ME DOING THAT IF I WERE YOU.

AT THIS, LIZZIE APPEARED TRULY SURPRISED.

OH NO! WHY DIDN'T YOU TELL ME BEFORE? WHAT HAVE I DONE?

MISS RUSSELL WOULD NOT FORGET WHAT SHE HAD SEEN.

THAT EVENING, EMMA BORDEN, WITH PAIL AND BRUSH, WASHED THE BLOOD-STAINS FROM THE WALLS AND FLOORS OF BOTH MURDER CHAMBERS.

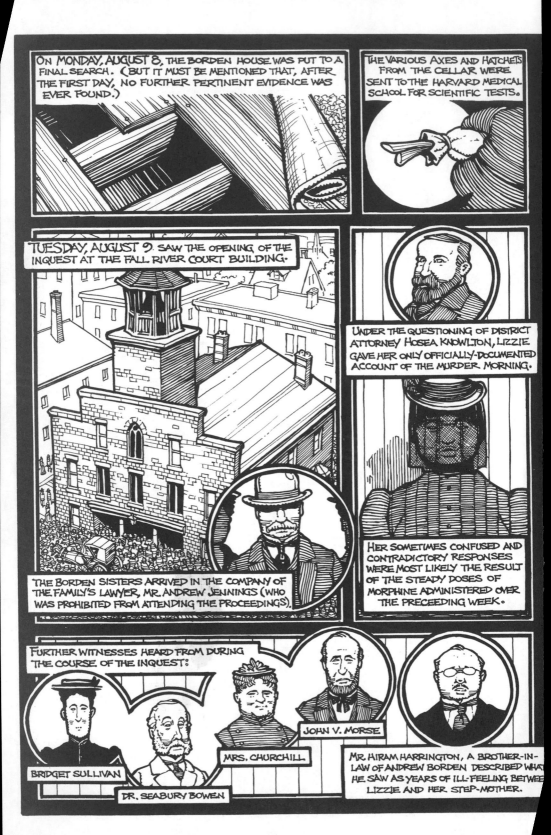

ON MONDAY, AUGUST 8, THE BORDEN HOUSE WAS PUT TO A FINAL SEARCH. (BUT IT MUST BE MENTIONED THAT, AFTER THE FIRST DAY, NO FURTHER PERTINENT EVIDENCE WAS EVER FOUND.)

THE VARIOUS AXES AND HATCHETS FROM THE CELLAR WERE SENT TO THE HARVARD MEDICAL SCHOOL FOR SCIENTIFIC TESTS.

TUESDAY, AUGUST 9, SAW THE OPENING OF THE INQUEST AT THE FALL RIVER COURT BUILDING.

UNDER THE QUESTIONING OF DISTRICT ATTORNEY HOSEA KNOWLTON, LIZZIE GAVE HER ONLY OFFICIALLY-DOCUMENTED ACCOUNT OF THE MURDER MORNING.

THE BORDEN SISTERS ARRIVED IN THE COMPANY OF THE FAMILY'S LAWYER, MR. ANDREW JENNINGS (WHO WAS PROHIBITED FROM ATTENDING THE PROCEEDINGS).

HER SOMETIMES CONFUSED AND CONTRADICTORY RESPONSES WERE MOST LIKELY THE RESULT OF THE STEADY DOSES OF MORPHINE ADMINISTERED OVER THE PRECEEDING WEEK.

FURTHER WITNESSES HEARD FROM DURING THE COURSE OF THE INQUEST:

BRIDGET SULLIVAN

DR. SEABURY BOWEN

MRS. CHURCHILL

JOHN V. MORSE

MR. HIRAM HARRINGTON, A BROTHER-IN-LAW OF ANDREW BORDEN, DESCRIBED WHAT HE SAW AS YEARS OF ILL-FEELING BETWEEN LIZZIE AND HER STEP-MOTHER.

ON THURSDAY, AUGUST 11, (ONE WEEK AFTER THE MURDERS), THE INQUEST STOOD ADJOURNED.

WITH THE TOWN NEAR HYSTERIA, LIZZIE BORDEN WAS PLACED UNDER ARREST BY MARSHAL HILLIARD.

SHE WAS ALLOWED TO SPEND ONE FINAL NIGHT IN HER HOME . . .

AND, ON FRIDAY, AUGUST 12, SHE RETURNED WITH MR. JENNINGS TO ENTER A FORMAL PLEA OF "NOT GUILTY."

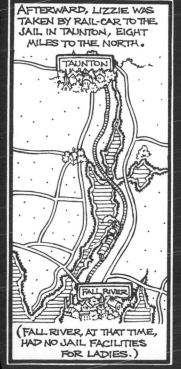

AFTERWARD, LIZZIE WAS TAKEN BY RAIL-CAR TO THE JAIL IN TAUNTON, EIGHT MILES TO THE NORTH.

TAUNTON

FALL RIVER

(FALL RIVER, AT THAT TIME, HAD NO JAIL FACILITIES FOR LADIES.)

THERE SHE REMAINED, IN A SMALL CELL, FOR THE NEXT NINE DAYS

UNTIL RETURNED FOR THE PRELIMINARY HEARING . . .

WHICH CONVENED ON MONDAY, AUGUST 22, JUDGE JOSIAH BLAISDELL PRESIDING (AS HE HAD OVER THE INQUEST).

THE HEARING, ALTHOUGH A RATHER PERFUNCTORY AFFAIR, WAS OPENED TO THE PUBLIC. I SAT IN THE PACKED, STEAMING COURT-ROOM FOR THE ENTIRE DAY.

MR. KNOWLTON CAREFULLY LAID OUT THE COMMONWEALTH'S WEB OF CIRCUMSTANTIAL EVIDENCE.

BUT DR. EDWARD WOOD, OF THE HARVARD MEDICAL SCHOOL, INTRODUCED INFORMATION BENEFICIAL TO THE DEFENSE.

A MICROSCOPIC EXAMINATION OF THE AXES AND HATCHETS FROM THE BORDEN CELLAR REVEALED NO BLOOD OR TISSUE RESIDUE, AT ALL.

THE AUTOPSIES PERFORMED ON BOTH VICTIMS SHOWED NO TRACES OF POISON OF ANY KIND.

BLOOD AND HAIRS ON ONE AXE WERE FOUND TO BE THOSE OF A COW.

DR. WOOD

THE DAY CONCLUDED WITH MR. JENNINGS' RINGING SPEECH FOR THE DEFENSE.

THE HEARING RE-CONVENED THE NEXT MORNING LONG ENOUGH FOR THE JUDGE TO PRONOUNCE LIZZIE "PROBABLY GUILTY."

SHE WAS RETURNED TO POLICE CUSTODY, PENDING A MEETING OF THE GRAND JURY IN NOVEMBER.

THAT EVENING, SHE WAS REMOVED TO HER CELL IN TAUNTON.

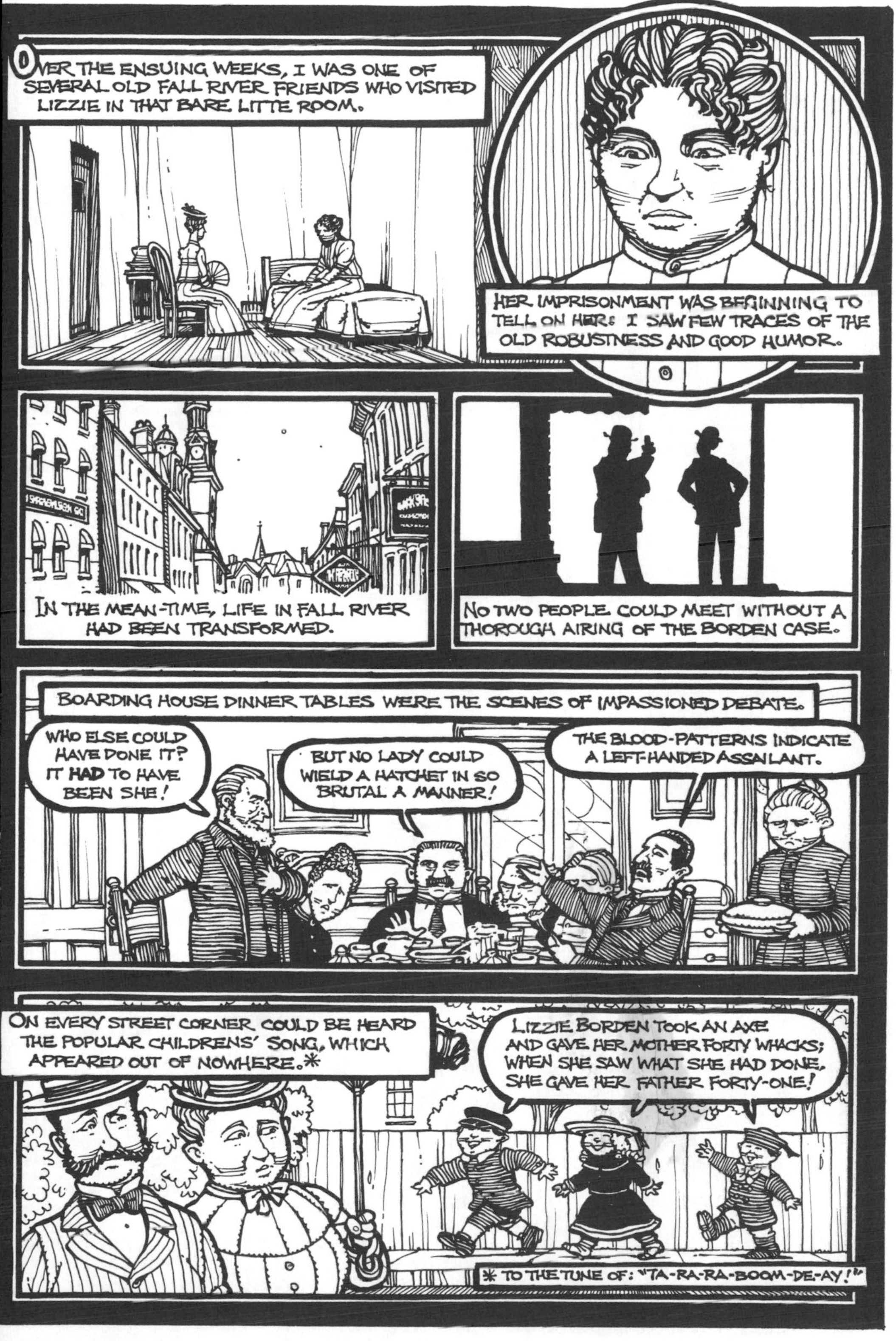
OVER THE ENSUING WEEKS, I WAS ONE OF SEVERAL OLD FALL RIVER FRIENDS WHO VISITED LIZZIE IN THAT BARE LITTE ROOM.
HER IMPRISONMENT WAS BEGINNING TO TELL ON HER: I SAW FEW TRACES OF THE OLD ROBUSTNESS AND GOOD HUMOR.
IN THE MEAN-TIME, LIFE IN FALL RIVER HAD BEEN TRANSFORMED.
NO TWO PEOPLE COULD MEET WITHOUT A THOROUGH AIRING OF THE BORDEN CASE.
BOARDING HOUSE DINNER TABLES WERE THE SCENES OF IMPASSIONED DEBATE.
WHO ELSE COULD HAVE DONE IT? IT HAD TO HAVE BEEN SHE!
BUT NO LADY COULD WIELD A HATCHET IN SO BRUTAL A MANNER!
THE BLOOD-PATTERNS INDICATE A LEFT-HANDED ASSAILANT.
ON EVERY STREET CORNER COULD BE HEARD THE POPULAR CHILDRENS' SONG, WHICH APPEARED OUT OF NOWHERE.*
LIZZIE BORDEN TOOK AN AXE AND GAVE HER MOTHER FORTY WHACKS; WHEN SHE SAW WHAT SHE HAD DONE, SHE GAVE HER FATHER FORTY-ONE!
* TO THE TUNE OF: "TA-RA-RA-BOOM-DE-AY!"

THE POPULAR FEELING AGAINST LIZZIE WAS NOT ALLEVIATED IN OCTOBER, WHEN THE BOSTON GLOBE (THERETOFORE HIGHLY RESPECTED) PRINTED A SERIES OF SCANDALOUS ARTICLES. SEVERAL NEWLY-UNCOVERED WITNESSES CLAIMED, AMONG OTHER THINGS:

OCTOBER 10, 1892

LIZZIE HAD A SECRET.

Mr. Borden Discovered It. Then a Quarrel.

Startling Testimony of 25 New Witnesses.

Seen in Mother's...

ON THE NIGHT BEFORE THE MURDERS, LIZZIE HAD INFORMED HER FATHER THAT SHE WAS WITH CHILD, AND THEY QUARRELED VIOLENTLY.

THE BORDEN SISTERS PAID A FANTASTIC SUM TO BRIDGE SULLIVAN FOR HER SILENCE.

LIZZIE WAS SEEN THE NEXT MORNING, PEERING FROM AN UPSTAIRS WINDOW, A HOOD OVER HER HEAD.

THE STORIES WERE SOON RETRACTED AS COMPLE[TE] FABRICATIONS — AND THEIR AUTHOR SHORTLY D[IED] UNDER QUESTIONABLE CIRCUMSTANCES.

LIZZIE CERTAINLY HAD HER DEFENDERS — AND THEY POINTED TO CERTAIN UNASSAILABLE FACTS:

NO MURDER WEAPON NOR BLOOD-STAINED CLOTHING WERE EVER FOUND IN THE BORDEN HOUSE OR YARD.

NO BLOOD WAS SEEN ON LIZZIE'S SKIN, HAIR OR CLOTHING BY THOSE SHE ENCOUNTERED ONLY MINUTES AFTER THE MURDERS.

SHE WAS SEEN IN THE YARD BY A PASSING VENDOR AT THE VERY TIME SHE CLAIMED TO HAVE BEEN THERE

MANY PEOPLE REPORTED HAVING SEEN A SUSPICIOUS-LOOKING MAN LOITERING NEAR THE BORDEN HOUSE.

LIZZIE SHARED A CLOSE BOND WITH HER FATHER — AND HAD NO DISPUTE WITH HER STEP-MOTHER THAT SHOULD HAVE LED TO MURDER

HAD SHE COLDLY PLANNED THE CRIMES, LIZZIE WOULD HAVE PLACED EVIDENCE ABOUT THAT WOULD POINT TO AN INTRUDER.

A NOTHER SCHOOL OF THOUGHT HELD THAT, IF LIZZIE DID NOT COMMIT THE MURDERS, HER ACTIONS INDICATE THAT SHE KNEW WHO DID — AND WAS, FOR SOME REASON, PROTECTING THE ACTUAL KILLER.

ALTERNATE SUSPECTS HAVE BEEN VIGOROUSLY PROPOSED:

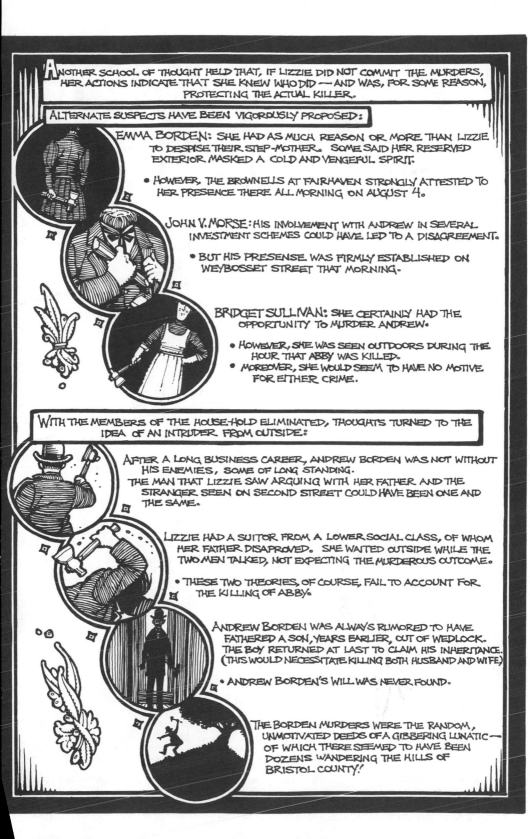

EMMA BORDEN: SHE HAD AS MUCH REASON OR MORE THAN LIZZIE TO DESPISE THEIR STEP-MOTHER. SOME SAID HER RESERVED EXTERIOR MASKED A COLD AND VENGEFUL SPIRIT.

• HOWEVER, THE BROWNELLS AT FAIRHAVEN STRONGLY ATTESTED TO HER PRESENCE THERE ALL MORNING ON AUGUST 4.

JOHN V. MORSE: HIS INVOLVEMENT WITH ANDREW IN SEVERAL INVESTMENT SCHEMES COULD HAVE LED TO A DISAGREEMENT.

• BUT HIS PRESENSE WAS FIRMLY ESTABLISHED ON WEYBOSSET STREET THAT MORNING.

BRIDGET SULLIVAN: SHE CERTAINLY HAD THE OPPORTUNITY TO MURDER ANDREW.

• HOWEVER, SHE WAS SEEN OUTDOORS DURING THE HOUR THAT ABBY WAS KILLED.
• MOREOVER, SHE WOULD SEEM TO HAVE NO MOTIVE FOR EITHER CRIME.

WITH THE MEMBERS OF THE HOUSE-HOLD ELIMINATED, THOUGHTS TURNED TO THE IDEA OF AN INTRUDER FROM OUTSIDE:

AFTER A LONG BUSINESS CAREER, ANDREW BORDEN WAS NOT WITHOUT HIS ENEMIES, SOME OF LONG STANDING.
THE MAN THAT LIZZIE SAW ARGUING WITH HER FATHER AND THE STRANGER SEEN ON SECOND STREET COULD HAVE BEEN ONE AND THE SAME.

LIZZIE HAD A SUITOR FROM A LOWER SOCIAL CLASS, OF WHOM HER FATHER DISAPROVED. SHE WAITED OUTSIDE WHILE THE TWO MEN TALKED, NOT EXPECTING THE MURDEROUS OUTCOME.

• THESE TWO THEORIES, OF COURSE, FAIL TO ACCOUNT FOR THE KILLING OF ABBY.

ANDREW BORDEN WAS ALWAYS RUMORED TO HAVE FATHERED A SON, YEARS EARLIER, OUT OF WEDLOCK. THE BOY RETURNED AT LAST TO CLAIM HIS INHERITANCE. (THIS WOULD NECESSITATE KILLING BOTH HUSBAND AND WIFE)

• ANDREW BORDEN'S WILL WAS NEVER FOUND.

THE BORDEN MURDERS WERE THE RANDOM, UNMOTIVATED DEEDS OF A GIBBERING LUNATIC — OF WHICH THERE SEEMED TO HAVE BEEN DOZENS WANDERING THE HILLS OF BRISTOL COUNTY!

THE GRAND JURY CONVENED AT NEW BEDFORD DURING THE WEEKS OF NOVEMBER 7-21...

AND ADJOURNED, AS MOST EVERYONE EXPECTED, HAVING ISSUED NO INDICTMENT AGAINST LIZZIE BORDEN.

BUT TEN DAYS LATER, THE GRAND JURY RECONVENED...

AND MISS ALICE RUSSELL TOOK THE WITNESS STAND.

APPARENTLY ABLE TO KEEP HER SILENCE NO LONGER, SHE TOLD OF WHAT SHE HAD SEEN ON THAT SUNDAY MORNING AFTER THE MURDERS.

...ZIE, WHAT ARE ...U DOING?

JUST BURNING THIS OLD DRES...

HER ACCOUNT WAS ENOUGH TO TIP THE SCALES OF JUSTICE THE OTHER WAY, FOR AN INDICTMENT WAS THEN ISSUED AGAINST LIZZIE FOR THREE COUNTS OF MURDER:

INDICTMENT
COMMONWEALTH
VS.
LIZZIE ANDREW BORDE...
MURDER.
...alth of Massachuse...

ONE COUNT FOR HER FATHER, ONE COUNT FOR HER STEP-MOTHER, AND A THIRD COUNT, CURIOUSLY, FOR BOTH TOGETHER!

LIZZIE WAS RETURNED TO TAUNTON TO AWAIT HER TRIAL — WHICH WAS SET FOR THE FOLLOWING SUMMER.

MISS RUSSELL'S REVELATION WAS ENOUGH TO SEVER ALL TIES OF FRIENDSHIP BETWEEN HERSELF AND THE BORDEN SISTERS FOREVER.

DURING THE INTERVAL BEFORE THE TRIAL, DISTRICT ATTORNEY KNOWLTON (WHO KNEW THAT HE HAD NO DIRECT EVIDENCE AGAINST LIZZIE) REFINED THE POINTS OF THE COMMONWEALTH'S CASE.

FIRST OF ALL, HE DISMISSED THE NOTION OF THE OUTSIDE INTRUDER:

NO WITNESS SAW ANYBODY ENTER OR LEAVE THE BORDEN HOUSE DURING THE PERIOD OF THE MURDERS.

NO INTRUDER COULD HAVE COUNTED ON THE CO-INCIDENCE OF JOHN MORSE BEING ABSENT, OR OF BRIDGET WORKING OUTDOORS, OR OF LIZZIE DALLYING IN THE BARN.

NO INTRUDER COULD HAVE SECRETED HIMSELF WITHIN THE HOUSE FOR THE NINETY MINUTES BETWEEN THE CRIMES.

IF THE INTRUDER THEORY ASSUMES THAT THE PRIMARY VICTIM WAS ANDREW, WHY WAS ABBY KILLED?

AS MR. KNOWLTON SAW IT, ABBY WAS THE PRIMARY VICTIM — BUT LIZZIE NEEDED TO DO AWAY WITH BOTH OF THEM.
- ABBY FIRST, OUT OF THE BUILD-UP OF A THOUSAND SMALL SLIGHTS AND RESENTMENTS —
- AND THEN ANDREW — FOR HE WOULD HAVE KNOWN AT ONCE WHO HAD MURDERED HIS WIFE!

TO OBTAIN A CONVICTION, THE COMMONWEALTH WOULD SET ABOUT TO PROVE THAT LIZZIE HAD:

- THE **DESIGN** TO COMMIT THE CRIMES, AS SEEN IN HER ATTEMPT TO PURCHASE POISON, AND IN HER CONVERSATION THE NIGHT BEFORE WITH MISS ALICE RUSSELL.

- THE EXCLUSIVE **OPPORTUNITY** TO COMMIT THE CRIMES.

- THE PHYSICAL **CAPABILITY** TO SWING A HATCHET WITH THE REQUISITE FORCE.

- **CONSCIOUSNESS** OF **GUILT**, AS EVIDENCED BY HER BURNING OF THE DRESS, AND HER DEMONSTRABLE FALSEHOODS CONCERNING HER WHEREABOUTS.

AS THE YEAR 1893 PROGRESSED, LIFE IN FALL RIVER BEGAN TO RESUME ITS NORMAL RHYTHM.

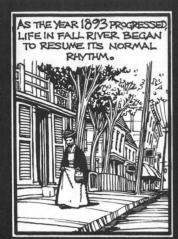

WHILE UP IN TAUNTON, LIZZIE WAS ALLOWED TO FURNISH HER CELL TO A RELATIVE COMFORT.

SHE HAD BECOME UNIVERSALLY CELEBRATED! EACH DAY'S MAIL BROUGHT GIFTS FROM WELL-WISHERS — AND EVEN PROPOSALS OF MARRIAGE.

ON MAY 31, ANOTHER HORRIBLE MURDER OCCURRED IN FALL RIVER.

A YOUNG WOMAN NAMED BERTHA MANCHESTER, AGED 22 YEARS, WAS CHOPPED TO PIECES IN HER HOME BY AN AXE-WIELDING INTRUDER.

THIS NEWS CAUSED MANY TO REVISE THEIR OPINION OF LIZZIE. THE VISION OF THE WANDERING MADMAN AGAIN INVADED THE PUBLIC MIND.

HOWEVER, IT MUST BE MENTIONED THAT THE MAN SUBSEQUENTLY ARRESTED — A DEVIANT PORTUGESE NAMED CORREIRO — HAD NOT YET ENTERED THE COUNTRY AT THE TIME OF THE BORDEN MURDERS.

AT LAST, LIZZIE'S TRIAL OPENED AT THE NEW BEDFORD COURT-HOUSE ON JUNE 5, 1893.

A PANEL OF THREE JUDGES PRESIDED

JUSTICE MASON   JUSTICE BLODGETT   JUSTICE DEWEY

MR. KNOWLTON GUIDED THE PROSECUTION, ASSISTED BY MR. THOMAS MOODY.

THE JURY

FOR THE DEFENSE, MR. JENNINGS ENLISTED THE AID OF MR. GEORGE ROBINSON, THE DISTINGUISHED FORMER GOVERNOR OF MASSACHUSETTS.

THE COMMONWEALTH CASE PROCEEDED FOR TEN DAYS.

THE TRIAL'S MOST DRAMATIC MOMENT CAME WHEN THE CLEANED AND BLANCHED SKULLS OF ANDREW AND ABBY BORDEN WERE EXHIBITED TO THE JURY.

LIZZIE, FEELING FAINT FROM THE SIGHT, HAD TO BE LED FROM THE ROOM.

MR. JENNINGS AND MR. ROBINSON WERE SO CONFIDENT OF THEIR DEFENSE THAT THEY PRESENTED ONLY A SMALL ROSTER OF WITNESSES :

THOSE PASSERS-BY WHO SAW THE STRANGE MAN ON SECOND STREET...

TWO MEN AND A BOY, WHO HAD EXPLORED THE BARN LOFT SHORTLY AFTER THE MURDERS (LEAVING AMPLE TRACES OF THEIR VISIT BEFORE THE ARRIVAL OF OFFICER MEDLEY).

BRIDGET SULLIVAN, WHO DECLARED THAT, IN THREE YEARS, SHE HAD OBSERVED NOTHING BUT CORDIAL RELATIONS BETWEEN LIZZIE AND HER STEP-MOTHER.

EMMA BORDEN, WHO INSISTED THAT IT WAS COMMON PRACTICE FOR BOTH SISTERS TO BURN THEIR OLD OR DAMAGED DRESSES.

I WAS AMONG THE THRONG IN THE COURT-ROOM WHEN MR. KNOWLTON AND MR. ROBINSON DELIVERED THEIR IMPASSIONED SUMMATIONS.

WHAT IS THE ANSWER TO THIS ARRAY OF IMPREGNABLE FACTS? NOTHING; NOTHING!

TO FIND HER GUILTY, YOU MUST BELIEVE SHE IS A FIEND! DOES SHE LOOK IT?

ON JUNE 20, THE JURY AT LAST RETIRED FOR DELIBERATION.

NOT GUILTY.

THEY RETURNED IN A MERE ONE HOUR AND SIX MINUTES WITH A VERDICT THAT SURPRISED NO ONE.

LIZZIE SOBBED QUIETLY, AS THE COURT-ROOM ERUPTED IN HUZZAHS.

NEWS OF THE VERDICT WAS RECEIVED WITH MIXED EMOTIONS IN FALL RIVER.

THOSE WHO THOUGHT IT A MISCARRIAGE OF JUSTICE KNEW, NEVERTHELESS, THAT NO MEMBER OF THE TOWN'S WEALTHIEST FAMILY WOULD BE CONVICTED OF ANY CRIME.

OTHER CITIZENS — MYSELF INCLUDED — FELT THAT THE CONTRADICTORY STATE OF THE EVIDENCE ALLOWED FOR AMPLE "REASONABLE DOUBT."

INDEED, I COMPILED AT THE TIME A LIST OF THOSE QUESTIONS YET UNANSWERED:

- WHY WAS ANDREW BORDEN'S WILL NEVER FOUND?   WOULD A MAN SO CAREFUL IN HIS FINANCIAL DEALINGS NOT HAVE PREPARED ONE?

- WHAT WAS THE PARCEL THAT ANDREW CARRIED HOME FROM HIS TRIP DOWN-TOWN?

- WHAT DRESS DID LIZZIE WEAR ON THE MORNING OF THE MURDERS — AND WHAT BECAME OF IT?

- WHAT WAS THE MEANING OF THE LAUGH THAT BRIDGET HEARD COMING FROM THE STAIR LANDING?

- WHAT CAUSED THE FAMILY'S ILLNESS DURING THE WEEK OF THE MURDERS?

- WHAT BECAME OF THE MURDER WEAPON?

- WHY WERE NO CRIES OR NOISES HEARD DURING THE COMMISSION OF THE CRIMES?

- WHY WERE THE VICTIMS FOUND IN SUCH UNNATURAL POSITIONS:

ABBY STRETCHED OUT SYMETRICALLY, AS IF ARRANGED THAT WAY...

ANDREW APPARENTLY FALLEN OVER FROM A SITTING POSITION, RATHER THAN RECLINING WITH HIS SHOES OFF, AS LIZZIE HAD RECALLED?

LIZZIE BORDEN RETURNED TO FALL RIVER A FREE WOMAN.

NEVERTHELESS, A CLOUD OF UNCERTAINTY HUNG OVER HER FOR MANY YEARS THEREAFTER.

THE BORDEN SISTERS SOLD THE HOUSE ON SECOND STREET AND PURCHASED AN ELEGANT MANSION ON "THE HILL," WHICH THEY CHRISTENED "MAPLECROFT."

A FALL RIVER JOURNALIST NAMED PORTER PRODUCED AN ACCOUNT OF THE CASE.

THE FALL RIVER TRAGEDY — E H PORTER

BUT WHEN IT APPEARED, LATE IN 1893, MOST OF THE EDITION WERE PURCHASED BY THE BORDENS AND DESTROYED.

DESPITE HER SOCIAL ISOLATION, LIZZIE USED HER NEW WEALTH TO ESTABLISH A COMFORTABLE LIFE FOR HERSELF.

AN ENTHUSIASTIC THEATRE-GOER, SHE SOUGHT THE COMPANY OF ARTISTES AND BOHEMIAN TYPES.

AT LAST, SOMETIME IN 1905, EMMA BORDEN MOVED FROM MAPLECROFT, AFTER A FINAL FALLING-OUT WITH HER SISTER.

PERHAPS THEIR MUTUAL SECRETS PROVED TOO MUCH OF A STRAIN BETWEEN THEM.

LIZZIE WAS LEFT TO LIVE OUT HER YEARS ALONE.

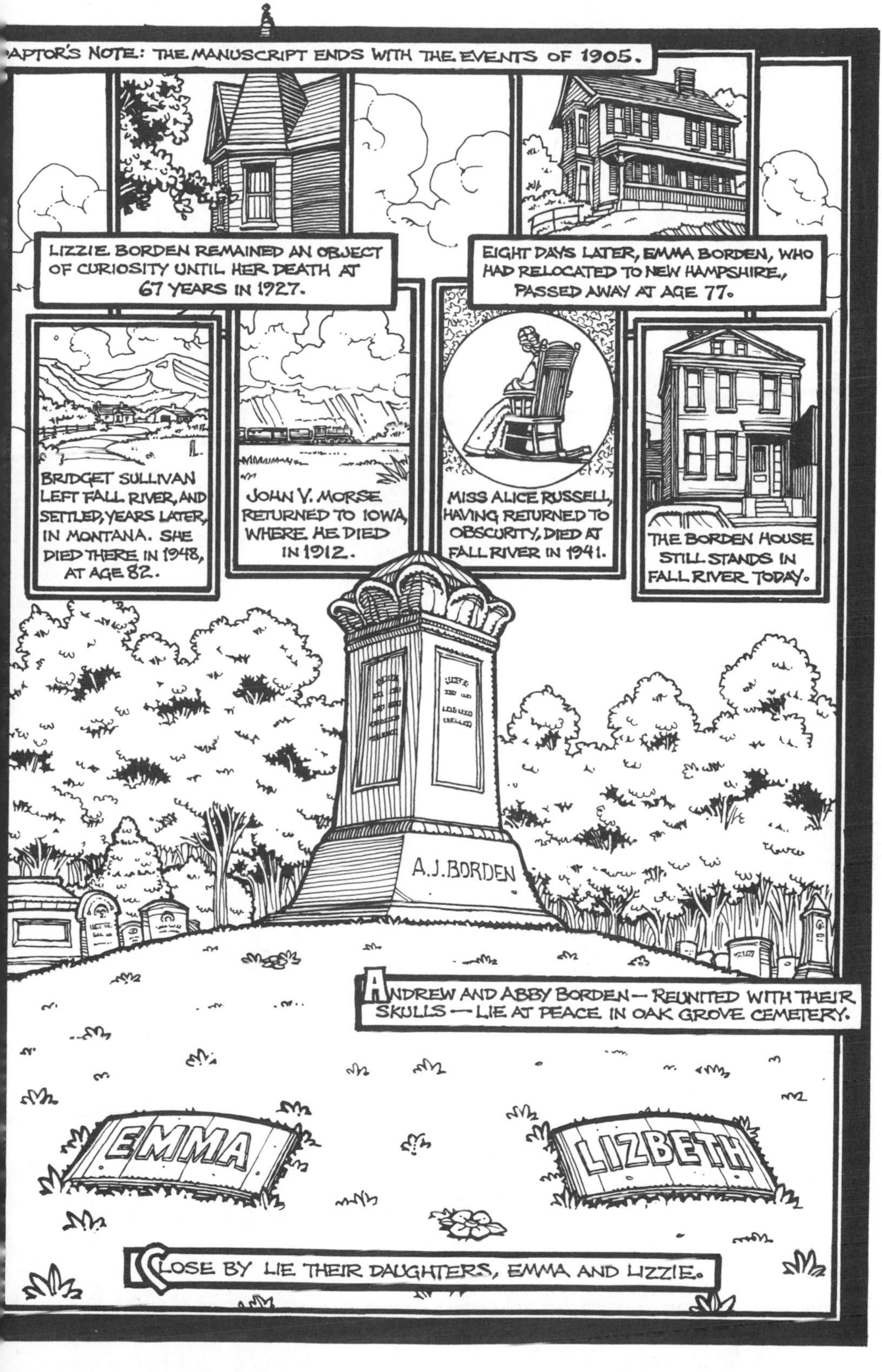

APTOR'S NOTE: THE MANUSCRIPT ENDS WITH THE EVENTS OF 1905.
LIZZIE BORDEN REMAINED AN OBJECT OF CURIOSITY UNTIL HER DEATH AT 67 YEARS IN 1927.
EIGHT DAYS LATER, EMMA BORDEN, WHO HAD RELOCATED TO NEW HAMPSHIRE, PASSED AWAY AT AGE 77.
BRIDGET SULLIVAN LEFT FALL RIVER, AND SETTLED, YEARS LATER, IN MONTANA. SHE DIED THERE IN 1948, AT AGE 82.
JOHN V. MORSE RETURNED TO IOWA, WHERE HE DIED IN 1912.
MISS ALICE RUSSELL, HAVING RETURNED TO OBSCURITY, DIED AT FALL RIVER IN 1941.
THE BORDEN HOUSE STILL STANDS IN FALL RIVER TODAY.
A.J. BORDEN
ANDREW AND ABBY BORDEN — REUNITED WITH THEIR SKULLS — LIE AT PEACE IN OAK GROVE CEMETERY.
EMMA
LIZBETH
CLOSE BY LIE THEIR DAUGHTERS, EMMA AND LIZZIE.

The Borden Tragedy

Press Clippings of the Time
and
Borden's Indictment

SHOCKING CRIME.

A Venerable Citizen and His Aged Wife

HACKED TO PIECES AT THEIR HOME.

Mr. and Mrs. Andrew Borden Lose Their Lives

AT THE HANDS OF A DRUNKEN FARM HAND.

Police Searching Actively for the Fiendish Murderer.

The community was terribly shocked this morning to hear that an aged man and his wife had fallen victims to the thirst of a murderer, and that an atrocious deed had been committed. The news spread like wildfire and hundreds poured into Second street. The deed was committed at No. 62 Second street, where for years Andrew J. Borden and his wife had lived in happiness.

It is supposed that an axe was the instrument used, as the bodies of the victims are hacked almost beyond recognition. Since the discovery of the deed the street in front of the house has been blocked by an anxious throng, eagerly waiting for the news of the awful tragedy and vowing vengeance on the assassin.

"FATHER IS STABBED."

The first intimation the neighbors had of the awful crime was a groaning followed by a cry of "murder!" Mrs. Adelaide Churchill, who lives next door to the Bordens, ran over and heard Miss Borden cry: "Father is stabbed; run for the police!"

Mrs. Churchill hurried across the way to the livery stable to get the people there to summon the police John Cunningham, who was passing, learned of the murder and telephoned to police headquarters, and Officer Allen was sent to investigate the case.

Meanwhile the story spread rapidly and a crowd gathered quickly. A HERALD reporter entered the house, and a terrible sight met his view. On the lounge in the cosy sitting room on the first floor of the building lay Andrew J. Borden, dead. His face presented a sickening sight. Over the left temple a wound six by four had been made as if the head had been pounded with the dull edge of an axe. The left eye had been dug out and a cut extended the length of the nose. The face

was hacked to pieces and the blood had covered the man's shirt and soaked into his clothing. Everything about the room was in order, and there were no signs of a scuffle of any kind.

SEVEN WOUNDS.

Upstairs in a neat chamber in the northwest corner of the house, another terrible sight met the view. On the floor between the bed and the dressing case lay Mrs. Borden, stretched full length, one arm extended and her face resting upon it. Over the left temple the skull was fractured and no less than seven wounds were found about the head. She had died, evidently where she had been struck, for her life blood formed a ghastly clot on the carpet.

Dr. Bowen was the first physician to arrive, but life was extinct, and from the nature of the wounds it is probable that the suffering of both victims was very short. The police were promptly on hand and strangers were kept at a distance. Miss Borden was so overcome by the awful circumstances that she could not be seen, and kind friends led her away and cared for her.

A squad of police who had arrived conducted a careful hunt over the premises for trace of the assailant. No weapon was found and there was nothing about the house to indicate who the murderer might have been. A clue was obtained, however. A Portuguese whose name nobody around the house seemed to know, has been employed on one of the Swansey farms owned by Mr. Borden. About 9 o'clock this man went to the house and asked to see Mr. Borden. He had a talk with his employer and asked for the wages due him. Mr. Borden told the man he had no money with him, to call later. If anything more passed between the men it cannot be learned. At length the Portuguese departed and Mr. Borden soon afterward started down town. His first call was to Peter Leduc's barber shop, where he was shaved about 9:30 o'clock. He then dropped into the Union bank to transact some business and talked with Mr. Hart, treasurer of the savings bank, of which Mr. Borden was president. As nearly as can be learned after that he went straight home. He took off his coat and composed himself comfortably on the lounge to sleep. It is presumed, from the easy attitude in which his body lay, that he was asleep when the deadly blow was struck. It is thought that Mrs. Borden was in the room at the time, but was so overcome by the assault that she had no strength to make an outcry. In her bewilderment, she rushed upstairs and went into her room. She must have been followed up the stairs by the murderer, and as she was retreating into the furthest corner of the room, she was felled by the deadly axe.

MISS BORDEN ATTRACTED.

The heavy fall and a subdued groaning attracted Miss Borden into the house. There the terrible sight which has been described met her gaze. She rushed to the staircase and called the servant, who was washing a window in her room on the third floor. So noiselessly had the deed been done that neither of them was aware of the bloody work going on so near them.

To a police officer, Miss Borden said she was at work in the barn about 10 o'clock. On her return she found her father in the sitting room with a horrible gash in the side of his head. He appeared at the time as though he had been hit while in a sitting posture. Giving the alarm, she rushed up stairs to find her mother, only to be more horrified to find that person lying between the dressing case and the bed

THE CROWD GATHERED AT 92 SECOND STREET

sweltering in a pool of blood. It appeared as though Mrs. Borden had seen the man enter, and the man, knowing that his dastardly crime would be discovered, had followed her upstairs and finished his fiendish work. It was a well known fact that Mrs. Borden always left the room when her husband was talking business with anyone. A person knowing this fact could easily spring upon his victim without giving her a chance to make an outcry. Miss Borden had seen no person enter or leave the place. The man who had charge of her father's farm was held in the highest respect by Mr. Borden. His name was Alfred Johnson, and he trusted his employer so much that he left his bank book at Mr. Borden's house for safe keeping. The young lady had not the slightest suspicion of his being connected with the crime. As far as the Portuguese suspected of the crime was concerned, she knew nothing of him, as he might have been a man who was employed by the day in the busy season. What his motive could have been it is hard to tell, as Mr. Borden had always been kind to his help.

Another statement made by the police, and which, though apparently light, would bear investigation, is the following: Some two weeks ago a man applied to Mr. Borden for the lease of a store on South Main street that was vacant. After a short time as Miss Borden was passing the room loud words were heard, her father making the remark. "I will not let it for that purpose." Quietness was restored in a short while, and when the man departed her father said: "When you come to town next time I will let you know." This was two weeks ago, but in the meantime the store has been let to another party, but why a person would commit such a brutal affair because of being refused the rental of a store is hard to see. Miss Borden thinks that the party wanted the store for the sale of liquor and her father refused. It was dark at the time of his calling and she did not recognize his features.

WENT TO SWANSEY.

At 12:45 o'clock Marshal Hilliard and Officers Doherty and Connors procured a carriage and drove over to the farm, hoping that the suspected man would return there in order to prove an alibi. The officers will arrive at the place some time before the man, as the distance is some ten miles, though it is hardly probable that he will return there. What makes it rather improbable that the man suspected is a Portuguese laborer is the statement of Charles Gifford of Swansey. Mr. Gifford says that the only Portuguese employed on the upper farm is Mr. Johnson, and he is confined to his bed by illness. Another man might be employed by Mr. Borden on the lower farm for a few days, but he does not believe it. An attempt was made to reach Swansey by telephone, but no answer was received.

A SIGNIFICANT INCIDENT.

Among the significant incidents revealed in the search through the premises was brought to light by John Donnelly, who with others searched through the barn to see if any trace of the fugitive could be found there. In the hay was seen the perfect outline of a man as if one had slept there over night. Besides this, it was evident that the sleeper was either restless or had been there before, because an imprint was found in another part of the hay that corresponded with the outlines of the first impression. Somebody may have been in the habit of going there for a nap, but the imprint was that of a person of about five feet six inches tall, and was shorter than Mr. Borden. This has given rise to the suspicion that the murderer may have slept about the place and waited for an opportunity to accomplish his deed.

ANOTHER STORY.

Another sensational story is being told in connection with the murder. It ap-

ANDREW JACKSON BORDEN

character was seen on Second street this morning who seemed to be on the lookout for somebody, and the police have a description of the man.

Marshal Hilliard, Officers Dowty and Connors went to Swansey this afternoon, but found the men at work on the upper farm who had been employed there of late. The lower farm will be visited at once. William Eddy has charge of this one.

At 2:15 o'clock a sturdy Portuguese named Antonio Auriel was arrested in a saloon on Columbia street and brought into the police station. The man protested his innocence and sent after Joseph Chaves, clerk for Talbot & Co., who recognized the man, and he was immediately released.

SKETCH OF MR. BORDEN.

Andrew J. Borden was born in this city 69 years ago. By perseverance and industry he accumulated a fortune. A short time since he boasted that he had yet to spend his first foolish dollar. Mr. Borden was married twice. His second wife was the daughter of Oliver Gray and was born on Rodman street. He had two children by his first wife, Emma and Elizabeth. The former is out of town on a visit and has not yet learned of the tragedy.

Mr. Borden was at the time of his death president of the Union saving's bank and director in the Durfee bank, Globe yarn, Merchants and Troy mill. He was interested in several big real estate deals, and was a very wealthy man.

pears that the members of the family have been ill for some days and the symptoms were very similar to those of poison. In the light of subsequent events this sickness has been recalled. It has been the custom of the family to receive its supply of milk from the Swansey farm every morning, and the can was left out of doors until the servant opened the house in the morning. Ample opportunity was afforded, therefore, for anybody who had a foul design to tamper with the milk, and this circumstance will be carefully investigated by the police.

Medical Examiner Dolan, who promptly responded to the call for his presence, made a careful examination of the victims and reached the conclusion that the wounds were inflicted by a heavy, sharp weapon like an axe or hatchet. He found the skull fractured in both instances and concluded that death was instantaneous. As to the blow which killed Mrs. Borden he thought that it had been delivered by a tall man, who struck the woman from behind.

A BOGUS LETTER.

It is reported that Mrs. Borden received a letter this morning announcing the illness of a very dear friend and was preparing to go to see her. This letter has turned out to be a bogus one, evidently intended to draw her away from home. In this case it would look as if the assault had been carefully planned. A suspicious

ABBY DURFEE GRAY BORDEN

The Fall River Herald

SENSATIONS in this city always move in cycles. It has been so for fully a dozen years. It will be a fortunate thing if the Borden murder is not followed by another tale of bloodshed.

THURSDAY'S AFFRAY

No Clue as Yet to its Per-
petrator.

POLICE WORKING HARD TO
REMOVE THE VEIL

Of Mystery That Envelops
the Awful Tragedy.

A POSTAL CARD THAT WOULD
SERVE AS A LINK.

Further investigation into the circumstances of the Borden murder shroud it
with an impenetrable mystery. Nothing
that has ever occurred in Fall River or
vicinity has created such intense excitement. From the moment the story of the
crime was first told to long after midnight
Second street was crowded with curious
people anxious to hear some particulars
that had not been told before.

ANDREW J. BORDEN.

Theories were advanced, some of them
plausible enough, but not one could be
formed against which some objection
could not be offered from the circumstances surrounding the case. Everybody
agreed that money was at the bottom of
the foul murder, but in what measure
and concerning what person could not be
conceived. That a bloody deed such as
that perpetrated in broad daylight, in a
house on one of the busiest streets
could have been so quickly and noiselessly accomplished and the murderer escape
from the house without attracting attention is wonderful to a degree. Nobody
was seen to enter the house by any of the
occupants, although all of them except
Mr. Borden were busy about the rooms or
in the yard.

WAS HE CONCEALED?

Could it be that the murderer was con-
cealed inside the dwelling and had awaited a favorable moment to carry out his
nefarious plans? The more the circumstances are considered, the more probable
becomes this view of the case. People
who have carefully examined the ground
believe that Mr. Borden was the first
victim, and that the killing of Mrs.
Borden was by no means unpremeditated.
Having accomplished the bloody work
downstairs, the murderer slipped stealthily
into the rooms above in search of the wife
and, finding her in the northwest chamber walking across the floor to the dressing
case, had crept up behind her without
attracting her attention and delivered the
fatal blow.

The plausibility of this view lies in the
fact that the fall of Mrs. Borden, who
weighed very nearly 200 pounds, would
certainly have jarred the building and
awakened her husband, who could only
have been sleeping lightly on the lounge,
as it was but a few moments after his
daughter had seen him quietly reading
there that the deed was done. Further
investigation confirms the belief that
Mrs. Borden was not chased upstairs by
the murderer because she was so near the
end of the room that she would have been
forced to turn and face her pursuer, and
the cuts on the head would have been of a
different nature.

Twenty minutes were all the time the
murderer had to finish his terrible work;
conceal the weapon with which he accomplished his crime, and conceal it in such
a way as to leave no traces of blood on the
carpet or through the house that would
reveal how he escaped; to pass out of the
house by the side door within 15 feet of
the barn where the daughter was engaged
and a like distance from the Buffinton
house on the north; pass the length of the
house and disappear up or down Second
street. John Cunningham was going
down the street about that time, and he
saw nobody pass him, and people who live
below saw nobody.

TALKS WITH INMATES.

There are no new developments in the
case to be gathered from the people in the
house. Regarding the servant, Bridget
Sullivan, a woman of about 25, it is pretty
well established that at the time that Mr.
Borden was assaulted she was in the attic
of the house. Her statement to the police
is as follows: "I was washing windows
most all of the morning and passed in and
out of the house continually. At the time
Miss Lizzie came down stairs I went to
one of the upper rooms to finish the window washing. I remained there until
Lizzie's cries attracted my attention; then
I came down and went for Dr. Bowen; I
never saw any one enter or leave the
house."

Miss Borden made the following statement to Officer Harrington as soon as she
was sufficiently composed to talk coher-
ently of the affair. It differs in only one
particular from the one she told Dr.
Bowen, namely, the time in which she
was out of the house and in the barn. She
said that she was absent 20 minutes, and,

upon being requested to be particular, insisted that it was not more than 20 minutes or less than that time. She said that her father enjoyed the most perfect confidence and friendship of his workmen across the river, and that she was in a position to know this, unless something unusual had happened within a few days. She told the story of the angry tenant, saying that the man came to her father twice about the matter, and that he persistently refused to let the store which he wanted for the purpose desired. The only vacant property of Mr. Borden was the room recently vacated by Baker Gadsby, and it is thought that this is the place the man wanted to use. Mr. Borden told the man at the first visit to call again and he would let him know about the rental. It is supposed to be an out-of-town man and that he called and found that Jonathan Clegg had occupied the store. It is also thought that the tenant wanted to use the place as a rum shop; this Mr. Borden would not allow. It may be added that the police attach little importance to this latter matter.

MR. MORSE TALKS.

Visiting at the house on the day of the murder was John W. Morse, a brother of Mr. Borden's first wife. He is fully six feet in height with gray beard and hair. He was not averse to talking, and said in response to questions:

"My sister, Sarah A. Morse, married Andrew Borden in the city of Fall River when both were, as I remember, in their 22d year. That was 47 years ago. At that time Mr. Borden was in reduced circumstances and was just beginning to enter business. They lived for years on Ferry street. They had three children, one of whom died when he was but three or four years old. The others, both girls, grew to womanhood and are now living; they are Emma L., aged 37, and Lizzie A., aged 32.

"Mr. Borden first went into the furniture business on Anawan street, where he remained for 30 years or more. My sister died 28 years ago. At that time Mr. Borden was worth fully $150,000, which amount he had invested largely in mill stocks, which were highly paying securities. He told me on one occasion that he had $78,000 in mill stocks alone. He afterwards invested heavily in a horsecar line, but now I am ahead of my story.

"About 20 years ago I went out west, and settled at Hastings Mills, Ia. On the 14th of of April two years ago I returned home, and since last February I have been staying with a butcher by the name of Davis, in the little town of South Dartmouth, which is near New Bedford. Yes, I am a bachelor. I have a sister living in this city. She married Joseph Morse, a second cousin. I have also one brother whose name is William, who lives at Excelsior, Minn. He is 65 years of age.

"Wednesday I came here from New Bedford early in the afternoon. I left that city on the 12:35 train, which arrived here about 1:30 o'clock. I walked from the station up to the house and rang the front door bell. Mrs. Borden opened it. She welcomed me and I went in. Andrew was then reclining on the sofa in about the position he was found murdered. He looked up and laughed saying, 'Hullo, John, is that you? Have you been to dinner?' I replied in the negative. Mrs. Borden interrupted Mr. Borden, saying: 'Sit right down, we are just through and everything is hot on the stove. It won't cost us a mite of trouble.' They sat by my side through dinner, and then I told them I was going over to Kirby's stable and get a team to drive over to Luther's. I invited Andrew to go, but he declined, saying he didn't feel well enough. He asked me to bring him over some eggs from his farm which is there located. I returned from the ride about 8:30 o'clock and we sat up until about 10 o'clock. Then Mr. Borden showed me to my room, his wife having previously retired, and bade me good night. That was the last I saw of him until Thursday morning.

"It was about 6 o'clock when I got up, and had breakfast about an hour later. Then Andrew and I read the papers, and we chatted until about 9 o'clock. I am not positive as to the exact time, and it may have been only 8:45 o'clock. While at the table I asked Andrew why he did not buy Gould's yacht for $200,000, at which price it was advertised, and he laughed, saying what little good it would do him if he really did have it. We also talked about business. I had come to Fall River, for one reason, to buy a pair of oxen for Butcher Davis, with whom I lived. He had wanted them, and I had agreed to take them on a certain day, but had not done so. Andrew told me when I was ready to go after them to write him at the farm, which would save him bothering in the matter. When I left the house I started for the postoffice. I walked down Second street, and, stopping in, got a postal card and wrote to William Vinnicum of South Swansey. I dropped it in the office and then went out of the north door of the building to Bedford street, and thence on to Third street, to Pleasant, to Weybosset street. I stopped there at the house of my cousin, Daniel Emery, No. 4; I went there to see my nephew and niece, the former of whom I found away. There I remained until 11:30 or 11:45 and then I started back to Borden's, as I had been asked there to dinner. I hailed a car going by and rode to Second street and thence I walked to the house.

"When I entered the premises I did not go by the front door. On the contrary, I walked around behind the house and picked some pears. Then I went in the back door. Bridget then told me that Mr. and Mrs. Borden had been murdered. I opened the sitting-room door and found a number of people, including the doctors. I entered, but only glanced once at the body. No, I did not look closely enough to be able to describe it. Then I went upstairs and took a similar hasty view of the dead woman. Everything is confusion, however, and I recall very little of what took place."

THE MEDICAL EXAMINER.

Dr. Dolan was called upon after the autopsy, but he had no further facts to disclose. He described the wounds and said that death must have been almost instantaneous in both cases after the first blow. Acting upon the rumor about the poisoned milk, the doctor took samples of it and saved the soft parts of the body for further analysis. He was of the opinion that the wounds were inflicted by a hatchet or a cleaver, and by a person who could strike a blow heavy enough to crush in the skull. In the autopsy, Drs. Coughlin, Dedrick, Leary, Gunning, Dutra, Tourtellot, Peckham and Bowen assisted.

NOTES.

John J. Maher was on a street car on New Boston road Thursday afternoon rather under the influence of liquor. He was telling that when a reward was offered for the man he could find him in 15 minutes. When questioned by an officer as to what he really knew, Maher said that a boy had seen a small man with a dark moustache come out of the house at the time of the murder and, going down Second street, had turned up Pleasant. Maher was locked up on a charge of drunkenness.

Officers Doherty and Harrington have been on continuous duty since the case was reported.

It was rather warm for the officers who were detailed to hunt for the murderer's weapon in the loft of the barn, but they thoroughly examined every corner for the article.

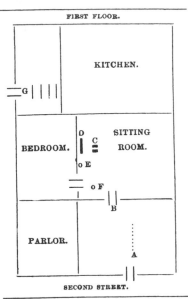

FIRST FLOOR.

KITCHEN.

SITTING ROOM.

BEDROOM.

PARLOR.

SECOND STREET.

A—front door. B—door to room where murder was committed. C—where the body was found. D—the lounge where Mr. Borden was lying. E and F—blood spots. G—back stairs and door.

ROOM WHERE BODY OF MR. BORDEN WAS FOUND.

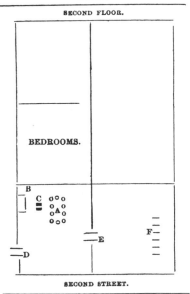

SECOND FLOOR.

BEDROOMS.

SECOND STREET.

A—the bed. B—dressing case. C—where body of Mrs. Borden was found. D—window. E—door to room. F—staircase.

WHERE BODY OF MRS. BORDEN WAS FOUND.

Officer Medley was one of the busiest men about town Wednesday night, and every remark or idea connected with the tragedy was thoroughly sifted by him.

When the news of the murder reached the people on the excursion it seemed too incredible, and a great many would not be convinced untill they reached home.

If interest and hard work in the case were to land the perpetrator of the crime into custody Assistant Marshal Fleet would have the man behind the bars long before now.

Every morning paper in Boston had a representative in this city Thursday night, and as a result the telegraph operators were kept busy into the small hours of the morning.

The excitement attending the tragedy continued at blood heat throughout the night, and it required a number of officers to keep the street clear in front of the house up to midnight.

Among the many articles secured on the premises is a crowbar over three feet long and weighing about nine pounds. It was found in the shed by one of the officers. It appeared, at first that there was blood on it, and a hasty investigation by two or three policemen convinced the finder that the substance with which it was spotted was blood. It was consequently brought to the police station, where it was found that the spots were nothing else than a few drops of paint and rust.

MORSE'S NIECE.

Mrs. Emery, upon whom Mr. Morse called, was disposed to talk freely to Officer Medley, who interviewed her Thursday night. She said in reply to questions that she had several callers during the day, and that one of them was John Morse.

"Was Morse the name we heard?" asked the officer of a companion.

"Yes," retorted Mrs. Emery quickly, "Morse was the man. He left here at 11:30 o'clock this morning."

"Then you noticed the time?" observed the officer.

"Oh, yes," was the reply, "I noticed the time.

"How did you fix it?" was the next question.

After some little hesitation, Mrs. Emery said that one of her family was sick, and that Dr. Bowen was her physician. "Dr. Bowen came in just as Mr. Morse left."

"Did they meet?" queried the officers.

"No, they did not," said Mrs. Emery.

At this point the niece in question entered the room and corroborated Mrs. Emery's statements, though both women finally fixed upon 11:20 as the exact time of Mr. Morse's departure.

Mrs. Emery volunteered information that Mr. Morse was well-to-do, at least she supposed he was comfortably off and that he had come east to spend his money. She was not positive on this point, however. Morse's niece was asked if she had ever seen her uncle before, and replied that she had. She had met him when she was five years old, and three weeks ago he had taken her from the cars at Warren to the Borden farm, Swansey.

THE OLDEST DAUGHTER.

Miss Emma Borden, who had been visiting in Fairhaven, returned home Thursday evening, having been summoned by the news of the crime. The details of the murder had not been told to her, and she was overcome by the recital. She is the oldest daughter of Andrew Borden by his first wife. All through the early hours of the evening the street was crowded with people, none of whom was admitted to the premises until they had disclosed the nature of their business.

A watch surrounded the house all night, and officers were on guard inside. No further developments were reported. The family retired soon after 10 o'clock and all was in darkness. Undertaker Winward had taken charge of the remains at the request of Miss Borden, and will prepare them for burial.

THE THEORIES DISCUSSED.

Today nothing but the murder was talked about on the streets, and the interest continues to be intense. The announcement that the family had offered a reward of $5000 for the detection of the murderers was the only new item to be discussed.

The theories which were advanced by those who have been closely connected with the case agree in one thing, and that is that the murderer knew his ground and carried out his bloodthirsty plan with a speed and surety that indicated a well matured plot. How quickly the report that was gathered about the premises five minutes after the deed was discovered that a Portuguese had done it was scattered abroad after the murder is looked on with suspicion.

Detective Seaver and other members of the state police force are assisting the local department in its work, and the office of the city marshal is the busiest place in town. New clues are being reported every hour and officers are busy tracking the stories to earth.

Mr. Morse, the guest of the Bordens, is well known in this city where he was born and lived many years. People recall that he went west quite early in life and engaged in raising horses in Iowa. He was said to have had considerable success with his stock and to have gathered together considerable property. Nothing definite about his affairs is known other than that he had told friends that he had brought a train load of horses with him from Iowa to sell, and they were now at Fairhaven.

SIGNIFICANT DISAPPEARANCE.

That letter of which mention was made Thursday as having been sent to Mrs. Borden, announcing that a friend was sick, has since disappeared. The explanation that was given out was that after reading its contents, Mrs. Borden tore it up and threw the pieces in the fire. Bits of charred paper were found in the grate, but not enough to give any idea of the nature of the note. Nobody about the house seems to know where the letter could have come from, and since publicity has been given and considerable importance attached to it, it is considered probable that the writer will inform the family of the circumstances and thus remove suspicions.

Various rumors have been started, one of which was that Miss Borden had assured a friend last winter after a mysterious robbery at the house that her father had an enemy somewhere. A HERALD reporter interviewed a lady to whom it was said this story had been told, but she denied any knowledge of it. Another was that the axe had been found in the yard, but the police have not heard of it.

A TENANT THEORY.

Causes for the murder are arising so fast at the present time that it is nearly impossible to investigate them. Hardly any of them are of sufficient weight to put a person under the ban of suspicion, but all are being thoroughly investigated. The latest story is about a former tenant named Ryan. According to the information Ryan occupied the upper floor of a house belonging to Mr. Borden, and was so obnoxious that he ordered him to move. While notifying the people he was compelled to seek the lower floor to escape the torrent of abuse that was heaped on him, and when the family moved the remark was made that they would like to see him dead. There is nothing more than this in the matter, but as all acts or words in connection with Mr. Borden in the past are being looked into the affair was looked into and found to amount to nothing.

A MAN WITH A CLEAVER.

Griffiths Bros., the carpenters on Anawan street, tell a story which may have an important bearing upon the terrible tragedy. They were driving up Pleasant street about 10 o'clock Thursday morning, when their attention was drawn to a man who was proceeding rapidly along the sidewalk in front of Flint's building. Under his arm, with the handle down, he carried a cleaver entirely unlike anything they had ever seen. It was the size of the instrument that caused them to take more than a passing glance at it. To them it looked like a tool sometimes used by fish dealers. It had a rusty appearance, as if it had not been used for some time.

The man was dressed very poorly. He had no beard and was short in stature. As the weapon with which the deed was committed has not been found, the carpenters venture the opinion that the cleaver they saw was the means by which Mr. Borden and his wife were killed.

SOUTHARD H. MILLER,

one of the city's most venerable citizens, and Mr. Borden's intimate friends, was spoken to on the matter. He replied that as far as motive was concerned for the deed he could not answer. He had known Mr. Borden for over half a century, and his dealings were such that nobody could take offence with him. Having learned the cabinet making business, Mr. Borden applied to him in 1844, when the city hall was building, for a situation as carpenter, work at cabinet making being dull. Mr. Borden continued in Mr. Miller's employ for about two years. He was a generous, plain and simple man. The reason he went into the bank business was so that he could more handily manage the property of Thomas Borden, his uncle.

The building in which Mr. Borden was killed had been erected by Mr. Miller, and throughout all their transactions he had found him to be a man of his word. As far as Mr. Morse was concerned, Mr. Miller had known him but for about a year, and in that time he had seen nothing that would prejudice him against the man. Mr. Borden's daughters were ladies who had always conducted themselves so that the breath of scandal could never reach them.

As the reporter was leaving Mr. Miller's parlor, Mrs. Miller who was present during the interview, said that she had lost, in Mrs. Borden, the best and most intimate neighbor she had ever met.

CONTEMPORARY EMPLOYMENT OPPORTUNITY

The Boston Daily Globe

DISCOVERY!

A Woman Inquired for Poison.

Said That Drug Clerk Identified Her.

Strange Story Told by Lizzie Borden.

Members of the Family Are Shadowed.

Stepmother the Cause of Trouble.

Reward of $5000 Has Been Offered.

[Associated Press.]

FALL RIVER, Mass., Aug. 5.—The Globe will publish the following tonight:

"At police headquarters, Thursday night at 7 o'clock, Capt. Desmond was posting himself on the murder by reading the papers and receiving reports.

"Marshal Hilliard was busy with his men, and inquiry for assistant Fleet revealed the fact that he had gone to supper. In a few minutes Mr. Fleet returned, and then a conversation took place between him and the marshal. Officers Harrington and Doherty were given instructions and passed out.

"Within 30 minutes after that the most important clue yet discovered was in their possession.

"The two officers made their discovery on Main st.

"At D. R. Smith's drug store they got the first important evidence.

"They approached the clerk, Eli Bence, and from him learned that Miss Borden had been in the store within 36 hours past and had inquired for a certain poison.

"The clerk was asked to accompany the officers and closely questioned as to the exact facts relative to the time, the girl's condition mentally, the amount and quality of the poison she had bought, or called for.

"The officers then led the drug clerk to a residence on 2d st. where Miss Lizzie was stopping for the time being. The young man was not previously well acquainted with the young woman, but he told them that he could identify her at sight.

"He did identify her, and in the presence of the police officers informed them that she was in his place of business and made inquiry for a bottle of poison.

"Miss Borden's reply to this accusation, as well as the exact language which was used at the time, is known only to the two policemen and herself.

"The statement above made is absolutely correct, and was verified in every particular by a GLOBE reporter last night within 10 minutes after it happened."

POLICE AT THE DOORS.

Shadowing Everybody Who Comes and Goes at House.

FALL RIVER, Mass., Aug. 5.—In the closely shuttered dining-room of the Borden residence on 2d st. are the bodies of the victims of yesterday's tragedy, which will tomorrow with brief burial services be consigned to the grave.

At the front door is a police officer whose instructions are to pass no one into the

ROOM WHERE A.J. BORDEN WAS MURDERED
At left is the sofa where he laid. The door next to that leads to the yard, and the right-hand door leads to the kitchen.

house, unless in authority, without the consent of the family.

A second officer stands in a sheltered nook at the rear of the premises, for what purpose cannot be said. The rear fence is fully 25 feet high, and it could scarcely be scaled with the aid of a ladder.

Still a third sentinel is at the outer gate, his duty is to keep the sidewalk clear and open for travel.

A crowd of men, women and children are braving a severe shower this forenoon for the privilege of lingering on the street and watching the scene of the tragedy.

Among them are officers in citizens' clothes, who are instructed to shadow and follow closely any member of the household who may go out.

Very little of importance has transpired around the house this morning. The family were astir at 6.30 o'clock, and about an hour later breakfast was served. There were the Misses Borden, Mr. Morse and a lady friend of the daughters present, and from the statements of the servant girl, Bridget Sullivan, they ate but little and talked less.

Miss Emma Borden, who was absent from home at the time of the tragedy, returned late yesterday afternoon. She appears very calm and self possessed, and was seen this morning and interviewed by officers in the case. Miss Lizzie has not yet decided to speak

for publication, and has denied all press visitors an interview. The city marshal will call on her today and take her statement, together with that of the servant.

The details of the funeral have not been arranged as yet, but will be before the day ends.

It is becoming well settled that there was

Not Perfect Harmony

in the Borden household.

It is said Lizzie and her stepmother never got along together peacefully, and that for a considerable time back they have not spoken.

When seen this morning, however, Mr. Morse denied the story, saying Lizzie and Mrs. Borden were always friendly.

Mr. Morse made his first appearance about 8 o'clock. He had a basket in his hand, and was evidently on his way to a store. He walked down 2d st. with a policeman at his heels, and soon after returned and went indoors.

He came out later on another errand, and again was trailed by the sleuth-hound of the law.

Then he stayed indoors until noon.

The writer has the assurance of the chief of police that no move will be made by his department until after the funeral tomorrow. Then the procedure will depend upon a combination of circumstances that are now being investigated.

LIZZIE BORDEN UNDER ARREST.

Fall River Police Take Her in Custody, Charged with the Murder of Her Father and Stepmother.

UTTER COLLAPSE OF THE PRISONER.

When the Warrant Was Shown Her the Accused Woman Lost Her Nerve and Was Taken to the Matron's Room Instead of a Cell.

REFUSED TO MAKE EXPLANATIONS.

Confronted by Witnesses Who Told Damaging Stories About Her She Declined to Say Anything Further——To Be Taken Into Court To-Day.

[BY TELEGRAPH TO THE HERALD.]

FALL RIVER, Mass., August 11, 1892.—Lizzie A. Borden, the younger daughter of Andrew J. Borden, was arrested at ten minutes past seven o'clock to-night charged with the murder and inhuman butchery of her father and mother.

This long expected and much predicted climax in the strange Borden mystery occurred in the courtroom over the central police station, where all the afternoon the inquiry into the murder had gone on with Lizzie Borden as the leading witness.

The wonderful courage and self-possession that have sustained this extraordinary woman abandoned her in her chief hour of need. Very likely she had not been without some expectation that possibly such a fate was in store for her, yet at the reading of the warrant she fell into a fit of abject and pitiable terror. A fit of violent trembling seized her, and so complete was the collapse of her physical system, weakened, no doubt, by the prolonged and terrible strain, that instead of the cell that had been prepared for her the matron's room in the central station was made her prison.

She is there now under close guard and lock and key. Ten minutes after the poor trembling, half fainting creature had been almost carried into these quarters she could hear the newsboys in the streets crying the news of her arrest, and the solution of the mystery and the clattering feet of the people who thronged to the station house with the hope of catching a glimpse of her.

THE NEXT STEP.

The next step in the procedure will be to bring her before the committing magistrate, who, in this case, is Judge Blaisdell. Under the Massachusetts law, either side has in such cases opportunity to move for a continuance of the hearing to any date within two weeks. In this case the State will undoubtedly ask for such a continuance, which will be granted, and in the meantime Lizzie Borden will be a close prisoner in the matron's room, if her condition demands it.

The arrest had been expected all day. Lizzie Borden and her sister were brought down to the inquest again to continue their testimony. Instead of arrest what was wanted of her just then was to give her a last chance to explain some of the circumstances that look so black against her and the discrepancies in her statement.

She found there Bridget Sullivan, Eli Bence, the clerk from Smith's drug store, from whom she tried to buy poison; another drug clerk, Frank Kilroy by name, and Medical Student Fred Hart.

SHE SAID NOTHING.

Lizzie did not say anything, and still paid no heed to what was going on about her. Emma Borden looked into her sister's face, and the tears began to run down her face, but she did not say anytuing. Mr. Jennings addressed a few words of hope and comfort to his unfortunate client and bade her goodby. Emma Borden went with her. She did not kiss her sister or even bid her goodby, but went crying down stairs and through the police guard room filled with curious people.

I don't think she saw any of them, hard as they stared at her. Then, still accompanied by Mr. Jennings and Mrs. Brigham, she went home. where she is now save one the only inmate of the household who was there eight days ago.

During the afternoon by the Chief's orders one of the matrons had fitted up one of the cells down stairs for Lizzie's reception, but as the Chief stood and looked at her, after the serving of the warrant, he concluded that a cell was no place for a human being so crushed and broken. He gave orders instead that she should occupy the matron's sleeping room, a large, well furnished apartment on the second floor.

Matron Russell had been summoned as soon as the arrest was made. She now led Lizzie into the room which is to be her prison quarters.

Up to this time the girl had not said a word nor indicated in any way a consciousness of her position. She arose and, the matron taking her arm, they walked away together. She was taken ill and the matron placed her upon a couch.

After a time she recovered some of that impenetrable bearing she had shown, though she was far from the Lizzie Borden of old. She would not converse much with the good hearted matron and soon went to bed.

PRELIMINARY EXAMINATION.

To-morrow she is to be arraigned before Judge Blaisdell for examination to determine whether there is evidence enough to have her committed to the Grand Jury.

The law in this State allows a wide latitude for preliminary examinations. The State is probably not well prepared to go ahead. Mr. Borden's safe has not been opened yet. No doubt there is other evidence the authorities will want to develop. District Attorney Knowlton will probably ask for a continuance for ten days or two weeks, which will be granted, and the prisoner will be remanded without bail.

If, when examination takes place, Judge Blaisdell does not think there is enough evidence against her to warrant the Grand Jury's investigation, he will discharge her. In that case she will have no ground for action against Hillyard nor anybody else. If the action of the Grand Jury is invoked she may be indicted in September and come to trial during the winter.

Her counsel, Mr. Jennings, refuses to give any opinion about the turn the case has taken, nor will he offer any reply to the charges against his client.

INDICTMENT.

COMMONWEALTH
VS.
LIZZIE ANDREW BORDEN.

MURDER.

Commonwealth of Massachusetts.

BRISTOL SS. At the Superior Court begun and holden at Taunton within and for said County of Bristol, on the first Monday of November, in the year of our Lord one thousand eight hundred and ninety-two.

The Jurors for the said Commonwealth, on their oath present,—That Lizzie Andrew Borden of Fall River in the County of Bristol, at Fall River in the County of Bristol, on the fourth day of August in the year eighteen hundred and ninety-two, in and upon one Andrew Jackson Borden, feloniously, wilfully and of her malice aforethought, an assault did make, and with a certain weapon, to wit, a sharp cutting instrument, the name and a more particular description of which is to the Jurors unknown, him, the said Andrew Jackson Borden feloniously, wilfully and of her malice aforethought, did strike, cut, beat and bruise, in and upon the head of him, the said Andrew Jackson Borden, giving to him, the said Andrew Jackson Borden, by the said striking, cutting, beating and bruising, in and upon the head of him, the said Andrew Jackson Borden, divers, to wit, ten mortal wounds, of which said mortal wounds the said Andrew Jackson Borden then and there instantly died.

And so the Jurors aforesaid, upon their oath aforesaid, do say, that the said Lizzie Andrew Borden, the said Andrew Jackson Borden, in manner and form aforesaid, then and there feloniously, wilfully and of her malice aforethought did kill and murder; against the peace of said Commonwealth and contrary to the form of the statute in such case made and provided.

A true bill.

HENRY A. BODMAN,

HOSEA M. KNOWLTON,　　　　　　　　　Foreman of the Grand Jury.

District Attorney.

Bristol ss. On this second day of December, in the year eighteen hundred and ninety-two, this indictment was returned and presented to said Superior Court by the Grand Jury, ordered to be filed, and filed; and it was further ordered by the Court that notice be given to said Lizzie Andrew Borden that said indictment will be entered forthwith upon the docket of the Superior Court in said County.

Attest:—

SIMEON BORDEN, Jr.,

Asst. Clerk.

A true copy.
　　Attest:　　　　　　*Simeon Borden* Clerk.

LIZZIE BORDEN GOES FREE.

THE JURY NOT LONG IN REACHING A VERDICT.

A Scene of Tremendous Excitement
in the Court Room When the Verdict Was Announced — Cheers
and Waving of Handkerchiefs
—Tears Mingled With Joy.

United Press Dispatch to the REPORT.

NEW BEDFORD, June 20.— District Attorney Knowlton resumed his argument this morning in the Borden trial, and made rather a strong presentation of detailed circumstances to sustain his contention that Lizzie Borden first murdered her step-mother, as a result of hatred and jealousy, then murdered her father when he come home, because he knew too much about family relations, and she did not dare to let him live.

The prisoner watched Mr. Knowltan fixedly during his long argument. In concluding, Knowlton claimed the defence amounted to nothing. He closed at 12:05 with an eloquent appeal to the jury to decide as their consciences should decide.

Court then took a recess till 1.45.

LIZZIE SAYS "I AM INNOCENT."

At 1.45 the court resumed its session, and the defendant was given an opportunity to speak.

She said, "I am innocent, but I will leave my case in your hands and with my counsel."

Justice Dewey then charged the jury. He told them to disregard previous hearings and defined the different degrees of murder. He stated the presumption of innocence, which was increased by defendant's character. There must be a real and operative motive.

The judge concluded his charge at 3:09, and the jury retired.

NEW BEDFORD, Mass., June 21.—Lizzie Borden was yesterday afternoon at 5 o'clock acquitted of the murder of her father and step-mother.

The jury filed into their seats after being out about one hour and a half, and were polled on their return. Miss Borden was asked to stand up and the foreman was asked to return the verdict, upon which he announced "Not guilty."

After the verdict had been received, the district attorney moved that the other cases against Miss Borden be *nolle prossed*, and the order of the court was to that effect.

Justice Mason gracefully thanked the jurors in appreciation of their work and faithful service, and reminded them that the precautions taken with them, which may have seemed irksome at the time, were solely in the interest of justice, a fact which they undoubtedly realized now. The jury was then dismissed and court adjourned.

THE VERDICT RECEIVED WITH CHEERS.

The closing scene in the trial was in direct contrast with those which had preceded it. Heretofore all had been decorous and in keeping with the dignity of the most dignified court in the country. But when the verdict of not guilty was returned a cheer went up which might have been heard half a mile away, and no attempt made to check it. The stately judges looked straight ahead at the bare walls, Sheriff Wright was powerless, and not once during the tremendous excitement, which lasted fully a minute, did he make the slightest sign of having heard it. He never saw the people rising in their seats and waving their handkerchiefs in unison with their voices, because his eyes were full of tears and completely blinded for the time. Miss Borden's head went down upon the rail in front of her and tears came where they had refused to come for many a long day, as she heard the sweetest words ever poured into her willing ears, the words "not guilty."

"THANK GOD," SAID MR. JENNINGS.

Mr. Jennings was almost crying, and his voice broke as he put his hand out to Mr. Adams, who sat next to him, and said, "Thank God," while Mr. Adams returned the pressure of the hand and seemed incapable of speech. Governor Robinson turned to the rapidly dissolving jury as they filed out of their seats and glanced on them with a fatherly interest in his kindly eyes, and stood up as Mr. Knowlton and Mr. Moody came over to shake hands with counsel for the defense. When the spectators had finally gone, Miss Borden was taken to the room of the justices and allowed to recover her composure. At the expiration of an hour, she was placed in a carriage and driven to the station, where she took a train for Fall River, her home no longer probably, but still the only objective point for the immediate present.